WORKS AND DAYS

WORKS AND DAYS
BY HAMILTON WRIGHT
MABIE

NEW YORK: PUBLISHED BY
DODD, MEAD AND COMPANY
MDCCCCII

𝔘niversity 𝔓ress:
JOHN WILSON AND SON, CAMBRIDGE, U. S. A.

TO

MARSHAL HUNTINGTON BRIGHT

CONTENTS

vii

Contents

Contents

WORKS AND DAYS

❦

THE HIGHEST SERVICE
OF LOVE

AFTER all that has been said in so
many forms of speech, love remains unexplained and unfathomable;
we know its manifestations, its modes
of expression, its surrenders and sacrifices, but the heart of it we do not know;
if we could penetrate this mystery, we
should understand God. The mystery of God, which lies like a luminous
cloud about us, would be revealed if
it were possible to analyze and probe
to the bottom any pure human love.

Wherever love is, there dwells the
mystery of God; mysterious because
it is too sacred for the searching of
thought alone, and too vast for the

capacity of present experience. The touch of the infinite is upon it, and it shares the boundlessness of the infinite; for no time is set for its duration, and no limits for its growth. Age, pain, weariness, sorrow, denial, do not weaken it; and it faces death with sublime indifference.

There is an instinct in the soul of love which knows that it is immortal. There come to it at times the premonitions of eternity; it cries out for infinite capacity and limitless time. No language is adequate to bear the burden of its expression or to reveal the glory of its pure and passionate craving to serve, to give, to surrender, to be and to do for the child, the wife, or the friend to whom it goes out in a silent, unreturning tide. After it has said everything, it retreats baffled and helpless because it has left everything unsaid. Its constant pain is the burden of unexpressed feeling. Try as it may every form of speech known to men, and in its heart of hearts there remains the consciousness that the deepest and truest things have not been said. The heart of man has overflowed in song, in art, in noble devotions of word and deed, but the heart of man is still an unplumbed sea. If love were mortal, it could find a voice sweet enough and of adequate compass to convey that which lies in the depths of its being; but how shall the immortal put on mortality? When the Infinite, twenty centuries ago, put on the finite, and the immortal wore the garments of the mortal, the divine was compelled to hold back the most glorious part of its nature because there was no language among men fine enough for its purity or capacious enough for its vastness. Christ was not only the revelation but the veiling of the Father. If love were finite, it would not bear forever in its heart a deep sense of helplessness; it is ready to give all, do all, save all, but it can give only a cup of water where it would open a fountain, and plead and pray where it would gladly lay down its life. The pain of love is rooted in its immortality.

And as its pain of unexpressed feeling and devotion is rooted in its immortality, so also is its divinest revelation of itself. For the highest service of love is not to console but to inspire, not to comfort but to stimulate. In the wreckage of hopes which sometimes overtakes the strongest and the best, love alone finds a hearing, and brings that sense of companionship which is the beginning of consolation. Wherever darkness settles, there shines the light of love ; and when the smitten arise out of the prostration of grief, it is the leading of this light which they follow with steps that grow stronger as they struggle on. The sorrow of the world has always sought the heart of love as its only place of hope.

But love has a higher ministry ; its glory is not in service in hours of disaster, but in its noble compulsion to do and to seek the best. He loves best who demands and secures the highest from the loved one. The mother loves her child most divinely, not when she surrounds him with comfort and anticipates his wants, but when she resolutely holds him to the highest standards and is content with nothing less than his best. The immortality of love shines in a home, not when blindness shuts the eyes of the mother and wife, but when the clear-sightedness of her love reveals itself in the greatness of her demands and expectations. It is a fable that love is blind: passion is often blind, but love never. They who love are sometimes blind to the faults of those for whom they care, but not because they love them. When love has its way, it grows more clear-sighted as it becomes deeper and purer. Happy is the child to whom the love of a mother is a noble stimulus, and fortunate the man whose wife stands not for his self-satisfaction but for his aspiration — a visible witness to the reality of his ideal, and unflinchingly loyal not only to him but to it.

For love, being immortal, cannot rest in anything less than the immortal in another; it craves perfection because perfection is the sign of imperishableness; men gather up and carry the perfect things from century to century because these beautiful finalities of character, of speech, of art, of action, confirm its hope of immortality. He who truly loves is irreconcilable to faults in one whom he loves; they blur the vision which always lies in his soul, and in the beauty of which his heart finds undying freshness of devotion and joy of anticipation.

The wisdom of love, which is wise in exact proportion to its depth and self-realization, is shown in its exactions rather than in its indulgences. The ministry of consolation is divinely appointed, and love knows all its potencies; but love also knows that nothing is ever really lost in this world except oppor-

6

tunity; all other losses, however bitter, are for the moment. With this wisdom in its heart, love knows that it saves most when it saves life for those whom it loves; for life is not simple existence; it is growth, and the things which come with growth. He loves me most who helps me to do and to be the best and the greatest in any human relation, not he who says the most comforting things to me when death has interrupted that relation. That fellowship, if it was true, will survive the touch of death; but if I have missed the heart of it by accepting something less than the best it had to offer, who shall call back the vanished years and restore the lost opportunity? I part from my friends, but I do not lose them; what I lose is the growth, the unfolding, the task, the vision, the chance of love in this present hour.

" Send some one, Lord, to love the best that is in me, and to accept nothing less from me; to touch me with the searching tenderness of the passion for the ideal; to demand everything from me for my own sake; to give me so much that I cannot think of myself, and to ask so much that I can keep nothing back; to console me by making me strong before sorrow comes; to help me so to live that, while I part with many things by the way, I lose nothing of the gift of life."

CHARACTER AND FATE

THERE has always been a passionate protest in the heart of the race against that element in life which men call fate ; the play upon unprotected natures of those events, accidents, calamities, which are beyond human control. These arbitrary happenings are often tragic in their consequences ; they often seem wholly irrational ; they have at times a touch of brutal irony. In many cases one is tempted to personify fate as a malignant spirit, studiously and with malicious cunning seeking ways of wounding, stinging, bruising and poisoning the most sensitive souls. There have been human careers so completely distorted and thwarted that it has seemed as if the gods were jealous of men, and anxious to rob the greatest rewards of their sweetness and the noblest achievements of their fruit. So often are the prizes snatched from

the strong hand that had grasped them
that the Greek poets could not withdraw
their gaze from that irony which at times
appears to make human life the mere
sport of the higher powers. The gods
seemed to be mocking men by holding
out glittering gifts and then suddenly
snatching them away. And this play of
what appears to be blind force still has
its way in the world. The noblest cathedral is at the mercy of the earthquake;
the divinest picture or poem may be
turned to ashes in a brief quarter of an
hour; the misplacing of a switch may
wreck the most commanding intellect;
a moment's inattention may break the
happiest circle and cloud the fairest sky.

The conditions under which men live
have remained unchanged except as
human foresight and skill have changed
them; but in that simple statement lies
an immense change of point of view.
There are still mysteries in the ordering
of the world which have not been solved
and probably are insoluble in this stage

of development; but we have discovered that nature is our friend and teacher in the exact degree in which we learn her ways and co-operate with her. The area of what once appeared to be mere blind interferences with human activity and happiness steadily contracts; the area of beneficent and helpful relationship steadily widens. Men are now safe where they were once in peril; they are now masters where they were once servants.

Through what seemed the play of mere physical force there now shines the light of that great movement upward which we call development; that sublime conception which, as one of the most spiritual thinkers of our generation has said, has come to light just in time to save some of the finest and most sensitive spirits from despair. For that conception not only involves a progressive order working in the place of what seemed to be a blind force; it involves also a progressive inclusion of all human interests in a system vast as the universe and old as eternity, and yet mindful of each soul's welfare and growth. A vision of order slowly becoming clearer as all things work together for the good of those who obey, throws new light on what appeared to be the waste and sheer brutality of the past; and where we do not understand, we can wait: since we may rest in the assurance that we are not the victims of a merciless physical order nor the sport of those who have power but not righteousness, the willingness to hurt but not the wish to heal.

We are learning also that a very large part of the happenings and experiences which once seemed to come to men unsought are really invited, and are only the outward and visible fruits of inward dispositions and tendencies. Human responsibility is very much more inclusive than it appears to be at the first glance, and men are far more completely the masters of their fate than they are prone to believe or confess. In fact, in any searching analysis, the power of what

we call fate shrinks to very small proportions. It is our habit to relieve ourselves
of our own responsibility in small matters
by invoking the bogy of bad luck, and
in large matters by charging upon fate
the ill fortune which we have brought
upon ourselves. Many men and women
suffer themselves to be comforted and
deceived all their lives by these illusive
agencies or spectres of their own making.
The results of their own blindness, carelessness, lack of judgment, neglect of
opportunities, misleading egotism, are
quietly and persistently put to the charge
of luck or fate; and the self-fashioned
sufferer takes another step in self-decep-
tion by drugging himself with that most
enervating of all forms of consolation,
self-pity. Hosts of men and women go
through their lives without once looking
their deeds in the face or seeing themselves with clear eyes. They comfort
themselves with lies until they lose the
power of sight; they disown the fruits
of their own sowing.

No words have pierced this demoralizing illusion with more searching force than Emerson's great phrase, " Character is destiny." When a man perceives that he is living in a world of absolute moral order, witnessed alike in the obediences and disobediences of men ; that what he reaps he has sown, and that he can and will reap nothing else; that his career is shaped and framed by his own will ; that the great experiences which come to him for good or ill, for misery or blessedness, do not pursue him, but are invited by him ; that a man's spirit attracts the things which are congenial to it and rejects those which are alien — when a man perceives these things, he is in the way of honest living and of spiritual growth. Until he does see these facts and accept them, he deludes himself, and his judgment of life is worthless.

Few things are more significant than the slow and often unconscious building of a home for his spirit which every man carries to completion. When the birds build their nests, they have access to the same materials, but what different selections they make, and how far apart their methods are! Every one who comes into life has access to substantially the same material; but each selects that which belongs to him. By instinct or by intelligence he builds his home with unerring adaptation to the needs and quality of his nature. To the pure all things are pure; to the impure all things are impure. The unselfish construct a beautiful order of service and helpfulness about them; the selfish make their own places. Honor and confidence and rectitude are in the air when the man of sensitive integrity appears; suspicion, mistrust and doubt pervade the place where the man without character abides. Clean and comforting thoughts fly to the pure in heart; debasing fancies gather like foul birds around the man whose imagination is a home of corruption. If we look deeply, a wonderful fitness reveals itself between those we know well and their several fortunes. Calamity may bear heavily upon them, but the moral world they construct for themselves out of the substance of their own natures is indestructible. Life is august and beautiful, or squalid and mean as we interpret and use it; the materials are in all men's hands, and the selection and structure inevitably and infallibly disclose the character of the builder. As a beautiful woman furnishes her home until it becomes an externalization of her own ideals and qualities, and then fills it with the charm and sweetness of her own personality until it becomes a material expression of her own nature, so do we all silently, and for the most part unconsciously, form spiritual environments and fashion the world in which we live.

There are few sublimer promises in the Bible than that which the words " Light is sown for the righteous " convey but cannot contain. This sublime phrase points the way to that complete

freedom which the human spirit craves ;
that final emancipation from the forces
which it does not choose and cannot control, which marks the full maturity of
spiritual development. It promises the
gradual supremacy of the soul over all
accidents, happenings, forces and materials ; its final emancipation from all
servitude. As life goes on, fate grows
less and less, character grows more and
more ; the fields become more completely our own, and yield nothing which
we have not sown ; the correspondence
between our spirits and our fortunes
becomes more complete, until fate is conquered by and merged into character.
In the long run a man becomes what
he proposes, and gains for himself what
he really desires. We not only fashion
our own lives, but, in a very true sense,
as Omar Khayyám intimates, we make
heaven or hell for ourselves. It is idle
to talk about luck, fortune, or fate ; these
words survive from the childhood of the
race ; they have historical interest, but

they have no moral value to-day. No one can hide behind them or bring them into court as competent witnesses on his behalf. It is wise to face the ultimate truth which must sooner or later confront us: we make or mar ourselves, and are the masters of our own fates and fortunes.

TAKING HOLD

THERE are thousands of men and women in the world who seem to be living under a cloud of predestined failure; nothing that they touch turns out successfully; the very stars in their courses seem to fight against them. Now, out of this multitude there are some who are facing material misfortune by the operation of causes which they are powerless to control, and to whom, therefore, the only success is a noble and heroic acceptance of failure; but there are many more whose lack of success lies in themselves. They have lost their grip on life; they go through the motions of activity, but there is no heart in their work, no vim in their onset against obstacles. If the kingdom of heaven must be taken by force, much more must the earthly victory be won by bold, aggressive attack. No one can succeed who holds his work at arm's length and goes into it faint-hearted and presaging failure before he has struck the first blow. The world presents an apparently solid and defiant front to the man or woman who must find a place in its ranks, but it is aston-ishing how soon it makes room for a new-comer who does not sue for place and work, but takes both as if they be-longed to him. Aggressive faith in the success of character, aptitude, and pluck is contagious ; the man who has it soon communicates it to others ; the man who has it not need not expect others to create it for him. God appointed work for every earnest and self-respecting soul ; without work of some sort no man or woman can lead a respectable life in this world. God also appointed the rewards of work to follow after it as certainly as the harvest follows the sowing. The true farmer does not go into his fields faint-hearted and despondent, distrusting the march of the sun or the coming of the harvest ; he trusts implicitly that

Taking Hold

ordering of the seasons which has never yet failed, and he knows that for every unfruitful year there will be a dozen fruitful ones. Take hold of life in the same spirit; put out of your mind all thought of failure, and out of your heart the weakness that springs from it; strike boldly, and strike strongly, with full faith in yourself, your destiny, and God!

LOOKING AHEAD

THE story of the unhappy woman who turned back in her flight from destruction, and remained forever transfixed, teaches a universal lesson. There is no subtler temptation than that which prompts strong men to recall past weaknesses and former transgressions and to surrender to the feeling of discouragement which always follows in the train of such recollections. The memory of failures and sins ought to keep us humble, but they ought not to weaken us; it is a satanic immortality of evil which binds the load of remembered sins on the pilgrim's back so securely that neither the consciousness of the Divine love nor of genuine repentance can loosen and cast it off. This temptation to doubt the reality of sorrow for misdoings and of the infinite compassion which makes them, though they were scarlet, whiter than snow, comes to those who are best equipped for usefulness and most sensitive to their own shortcomings. Those who are really pure at heart suffer tenfold for their offences, and are the easy prey of the temptation which prompts them to turn back when their gaze should be forward.

Men are slowly reversing some of their old and false conceptions of life, and among them the thought of human life as a continual fall from a former state of health and soundness, rather than as a possible growth out of imperfection into strength and purity. We do not expect the calyx-covered bud to breathe forth the sweetness of the flower, nor the flower to possess the ripeness of the fruit. Neither should we look for perfectness, for full and rounded symmetry, in a development which moves slowly, stage by stage, through the long education of experience, to remote and final completeness. The golden age is behind us only in the heathen myths; in the Christian prophecies it always lies ahead. The lily is not less fair or fragrant because its roots are in the mud; its saintly purity is the whiter because of the transformation which it has wrought in the elements of its life. A human character, full of inspiration, drawn upward by all the impulses of its nature when they are brought into harmony and educated into strength, is not less noble because of the hours of weakness through which it has passed. If God's promises are true, the stains which it feels, and which others perhaps remember, are no longer visible to One who sees all things as they are. The sure defence against the temptation to be weakened by the memory of past sins is to look ahead; to feel that one's true life lies always in advance, and never behind; that out of weakness true penitence brings strength, and out of sorrow there may be formed a crown of joy.

WORKING OUT

THERE are dark hours in most lives, when the threads in one's hand fly into an apparently hopeless tangle, and the fair design that was beginning to discover itself is for the moment lost entirely, everything seems to turn to ashes, and one looks in vain for a ray of light to beckon him on through a darkness that has become impenetrable. These are the hours that try men's souls, and test their characters as by fire. If one has been buoyed up and sustained hitherto by favoring circumstances, his fall is almost inevitable; only the man of real fibre survives the withdrawal of all external supports. And yet it is just such crises as these that the comprehensive experience of life trains men to meet. The ship on the stocks is built for storms, not for fair weather. The best, the sweetest, and the deepest things which life has to bestow are missed by the very few whom the world foolishly calls fortunate, who escape all storms by the way, and reach the end of their journey without knowing whether the bark they sail in is a thing to master angry seas or merely a fragile craft which has made the voyage by chance.

But the darkness that surrounds men at times is more often apparent than real; it is a gloom which comes from an earth-born fog, and not from the extinction of the sun in the heavens. For most men there is an escape from the extreme sorrows of deprivation and loss; an experience rarely turns out so awful as it was in anticipation; in a sudden confusion of one's affairs there is, in most cases at least, a safe way out. A little patient waiting will often set right a tangle which seemed for the moment hopeless; a brave heart will breast the storm until it has spent its fury. But there is another and a better way of meeting one's difficulties; it is to look them clearly in the face, grapple with them resolutely, and work one's way out from under them. The obstacles that will not yield to steady work are few; inch by inch the greatest mountain ranges yield to the persistent storming of the drill, until an open passage is made through their mighty barriers for the use of commerce and travel. Work is a sovereign word in this world; a word which has the quality of mastership in it; a word of more magical power than all the old talismanic words of necromancy. If you have come to a dark and baffling hour in your life, if all things seem to conspire to bring you injury and loss, do not sit down in despair, but quietly and resolutely, one day at a time, set yourself to work out your own salvation.

SHARING SUCCESS

WHEN one realizes what life means in its higher relations and duties, it is pathetic to notice how constantly people apologize to one another for any small trouble which they impose. The young man who goes to ask the man of established position for a letter of introduction or for personal interest in securing an opportunity for work, almost invariably expresses regret for the interruption which his request necessitates; as if the world were wholly selfish, and any kind of service done to another were in a way exceptional and out of the common run of things! That a man shall put his strength, his time, and his ability into caring for his own is taken for granted; but if he is asked to do anything for any one else, he is thanked as if he were doing an unusual thing. As a matter of fact, the one duty is as close, as obvious, and as imperative as the other. The man who throws a door open to one who is waiting for an opportunity has done nothing more exceptional than if he had put an hour's work into the gaining of his own bread, or the clothing of his own body. He is simply doing what a respectable spiritual being might be expected to do. The making of opportunities, the throwing open of doors, is as much the duty of the man who has the opportunity as caring for his own family. It is, indeed, one of the highest rewards of success — if one understands what success means — to be in the way of putting others on the same road. Nothing is more spiritually vulgar and shabby than to climb up and throw down the ladder by which one has climbed. Nothing shows the true nature of a man more than the spirit in which he treats success. If he is mean and niggardly in his soul, he accepts it as a kind of personal distinction or gift,

and hoards it as a miser hoards money;
if he is generous, he spends it freely,
eager that others should share what he
has gotten.   And no man deserves success, or ought to keep it, who fails to
make this spiritual use of it.   He who
makes this use of it cannot be corrupted
by any kind of success or spoiled by
any kind of prosperity; he who fails to
do this was corrupted and spoiled before
he began.

THE SMALLER VISION

THERE are few misfortunes in life so
blighting as the loss of the power
of admiration. The man who can no
longer generously and unaffectedly admire a fine person or deed has suffered a
loss at the very heart of his life. He
may see a few near-at-hand and relatively
unimportant things more clearly than his
less critical fellows, but he has paid for
that small access of clear vision the terrible price of loss of large vision. He
sees the fence across the road more distinctly than his neighbor, but the great
ranges of the hills against the horizon
are no longer visible to him. The skeptical temper serves its purpose as a brake,
but the man in whom it becomes the
dominant temper ceases to advance; for
there is no propulsion in a brake. Such
a man is fast bound in a constantly

narrowing world; the springs which feed life are steadily drying up in him; the hopes which make life rich in spite of its apparent poverty are slowly or swiftly fading from his view. He is wise about small things, and ignorant concerning great things. He so accustoms himself to see the small imperfections, the petty incongruities, that he is blind to the noble growth which is steadily pushing on through these minor and passing blemishes to final perfection. Such a man sees the wart on Cromwell's face, but he never for an instant sees Cromwell; he is so overwhelmed by Mr. Lincoln's apparent lack of seriousness that he utterly misses the vision of one of the most inspiring careers in the history of the world.

The mind that becomes entirely critical is small without realizing its littleness, and is surrounded by nobler minds without comprehending them; it is as much without self-knowledge as it is without true knowledge of others. It makes a

The Smaller Vision

small, mean world for itself by selecting the petty imperfections of the great growing world about it, and putting them into a misleading order; an order which it uses as the base of a still smaller philosophy which deals with the seams in the garment of creation, but ignores the garment. It is wise to be critical of ourselves, for self-criticism is a means of growth; but humanity has too many sides to be put into the little cup of our individual knowledge, and the universe is too vast for our little measuring-rods. So long as there is a God, so long as men and women constantly rise out of weakness to such heights of nobility, and so long as Nature is clothed in such power and beauty, it is safer to revere than to judge, and wiser to admire than to condemn.

ON GUARD

THE great crises and temptations of life come, for the most part, when they are least expected. So also do the great opportunities. A young man fancies that, when his great chance comes he will have time for special preparation, like the athlete who knows the date when his endurance will be put to the test and subjects himself to thorough training. But such opportunities are rarely given. There is no preparation for exceptional opportunities, except that which a man puts into his daily work; the measure of his hourly diligence and fidelity will be the measure of his preparation for the great moment when it comes. Not less suddenly and without preparation come our greatest temptations, and this is the subtlest danger that lies in wait for us. In one sense there is no such thing as accumulation of character. It is true that the longer one remains pure and honest and true, the more steadfast and certain becomes the upward impulse of his nature; but there is rarely a day when the whole fabric of character is not put to the test by some new crisis, rarely an hour when the yes or no, which have been repeated so many times, must not be repeated again to some question involving right or wrong. No man can afford to live on his character as he lives on the capital which he has acquired in business, and it is this conception of character which has betrayed many strong men. Paul, who belonged to the order of strenuous workers, and in whose life there was no rest from struggle, seems to have been constantly haunted by the fear that, after all the good he had done to others, he might himself become a castaway. The same peril lurks in the path of every man, and no past goodness can protect him; character can be preserved only by a struggle in which there is no truce, armistice, or treaty of peace. Nothing but conquest, victoriously carried on till the field is cleared by the summons of death, can keep any man secure. He who falls asleep for a moment at his post often inflicts as great an injury on the cause he defends as the most unscrupulous traitor. If vigilance is the price of Liberty, much more is it also the price of safety and character and righteousness.

THE REAL PREPARATION

WHEN Wellington said that the Battle of Waterloo was won on the cricket-field at Eton, he was putting in a picturesque way a truth which many men learn too late; the truth that the victories of life are won, not on the fields where the decisive struggle takes place, but in the obscure and forgotten hours of preparation. Success or failure lies in the hands of the boy long before the hour of final test comes. Wars are won in times of peace in armories, foundries, training schools, and at staff headquarters. France was conquered, a quarter of a century ago, before a single German soldier set foot on her soil by the marvellous preparation which had been going on for years under the thorough German military and educational system. The student thinks he can waste his opportunities and still fit himself for the critical moments in his mature life by hard work when the hour strikes, by energetic special preparation when the time for action comes; but specific preparation is impossible to the man who has neglected general preparation. Knowledge cannot be picked up on short notice except by the man whose mind is already well stocked; a particular skill can be rapidly acquired only by the man who has thoroughly trained all his faculties. The thoroughly educated lawyer, with the power of attention and concentration which are among the best results of a genuine education, can readily familiarize himself with a new field of knowledge for a special use; but the half-educated man is unable to grasp, arrange, or command the facts. It is often said of speakers that they are unusually eloquent when called upon so suddenly as to be shut off from all possibility of preparation; and such speeches are called extempore, as if the word involved lack of preparation. It is safe to say that no man ever yet made a really good speech who had not made long, thorough, and painstaking preparation ; not specific preparation for the particular occasion, but general preparation for all occasions. It is the thoroughly trained man who shines when he is suddenly called upon ; under the pressure of the moment all his faculties come to his assistance, and into fifteen minutes of talk he condenses the thinking of months or years. Tap an empty man and you will get nothing ; tap a full man and you will get the best there is in him.

In the higher fields of success there are no accidents ; men reap precisely what they have sown, and nothing else ; they do well precisely what they have prepared to do, and they do nothing else well. This preparation is often unconscious, but it is not the less thorough for that reason. In fact, the larger and deeper part of preparation for the greater experiences and works of life is always unconscious. The cricketers in the field

at the English public school did not
know that they were fighting and winning one of the decisive battles of history ;
we do not know when we are making
ourselves strong, rich, and great in resource and character. The world puts
its force into us when we put ourselves
in right relation to it ; experience makes
us constantly wiser if we know how to
rationalize it ; time deposits all manner
of treasure in our memory and imagination if we hold the doors open. Nothing
is lost upon a man who is bent upon
growth ; nothing wasted on one who is
always preparing for his work and his
life by keeping eyes, mind, and heart
open to nature, men, books, experience.
Such a man finds ministers to his education on all sides ; everything co-operates
with his passion for growth. And what
he gathers serves him at unexpected
moments, in unforeseen ways. All things
that he has seen, heard, known, and felt
come to his aid in the critical moment to
make his thought clear and deep, his

40

illustration luminous, his speech eloquent and inspiring. "The poet, the orator," says Emerson, who was a man of this order, "bred in the woods, whose senses have been nourished by their fair and appeasing changes, year after year, without design and without heed, — shall not lose their lessons altogether in the roar of cities or the broil of politics. Long hereafter, amid agitation and terror in national councils, — in the hour of revolution, — these solemn images shall reappear in their morning lustre, as fit symbols and words of the thoughts which the passing events shall awaken. At the call of a noble sentiment, again the woods wave, the pines murmur, the river rolls and shines, and the cattle low upon the mountains, as he saw and heard them in his infancy. And with these forms the spells of persuasion, the keys of power, are put into his hands."

THE LIGHT OF FAITH

IF there were to be a new beatitude, it might well read, " Blessed are the cheerful ; " for to them is given the gift of diffusing hope and courage and joy. It is not too much to say that they are not only light, but life bringers ; for courage and joy prolong life, as discouragement and despair shorten it. Plants dwindle and die without the sun, and men grow old and perish without the warmth and cheer of hope and courage. If these qualities were purely temperamental, those who lacked them could not hope to possess them ; but cheerfulness is not only inheritable, it may be cultivated. A cheerful face is the outward and visible sign of an inward condition, and that condition may be secured by any one who is willing to pay the price of effort and steady purpose which the acquisition of any virtue exacts. It is as easy to cultivate cheerfulness as to cultivate patience or good temper or courtesy. These qualities society demands of every man, and if nature has not bestowed them on him, society insists that he shall cultivate them. The bad-tempered and discourteous person finds himself living in an ever-widening zone of silence and solitude; people do not care for his society, and are eager to give him exclusive enjoyment of it. In like manner, society ought to demand cheerfulness of all its members; the man who spreads depression and breeds discouragement ought to be ostracized, because he strikes at the very heart of the social life. Depression and despair are pre-eminently unsocial vices; and in so far as they are diffused, they sap social courage and drain the fountains of social happiness.

The depressed man, whose spirit kills joy and makes gloom contagious, owes it to his fellows to keep despair to himself, as a man suffering from a contagious disease owes it to society to keep his fellows free from danger. This often involves inconveniences and hardship, but inconveniences and hardship must be borne when the good of society is at stake. Sorrow longs for companionship, and ought never to be denied it; but sorrow and the pessimistic temper have nothing in common. Some of the most beautiful examples of cheerfulness which society has known have been furnished by those whose sorrows were more than their joys. Men need hope and courage for the power of growth and the peace of spirit which these noble qualities bring with them; and cheerfulness is, therefore, a duty which every man owes to his fellows. For cheerfulness and despondency are alike contagious. A discouraged leader can chill the bravest army ever put in the field; a buoyant leader can put resolution into cowards. The roots of cheerfulness are in faith; the hope which shines on the faces of some men and women is the reflection of the light which shines in the face of God.

MORAL USES OF MEMORY

THERE are many facts which indicate that nothing ever escapes the memory; that while the power of recollection may fail from time to time, the record, once made, although it becomes invisible, is made forever. It is probably inaccurate to say that a man ever loses faculty of memory; even those whose memories are impaired, in moments of great excitement recall vividly and describe accurately things which they were supposed to have forgotten. Every man keeps within himself an indestructible record of his own life. He may cease to be able to read it for a time, but this loss of power is apparently only for a time. The light of vitality may sink so low that the words written on the tablet of the heart become illegible, but when that light flashes up again they are once more distinct. If this be true, not only is the unity of life assured and the integrity of personality preserved, but every man carries with him the explanation of his own career and the record of his own destiny. There is something terrible and at the same time sublime in the text, " Thou shalt remember all the way which the Lord thy God hath led thee." When one comes to remember the things he would like to forget, the memory takes on the guise of an inexorable judge. It is, however, an unflinching friend. If it were possible to forget one's sins and blunders, the faculty of moral growth would be arrested. If one could go out of the old year into the new and carry nothing with him but the memory of agreeable things, without the consciousness of the failures, indulgences and weaknesses of the year, there would be neither the tonic of repentance nor the spur to better living. Our past is not bound to us as the ball is chained to the criminal, to keep us in a place of punishment; it is given to us to remind us that the only moral safety is in moral progress, and that the man who has made a moral mistake or committed a sin can never be sure of his safety until he has removed himself as far as possible from the scene and occasion of his weakness. The best thing about the memory of our evil deeds is the horror they give us of all associations with them, and the desire they create in us to remove ourselves from them as far as the ends of the earth. The best education of a year may not come from the things which seem happy in it, but from those which brought us at the moment the greatest unhappiness. There is no way of deciding what is spiritually fortunate or unfortunate at the time; our most grievous calamities are often seen later to have borne the fruit of greatest happiness, and what appeared to be at the moment our largest prosperities have turned later to ashes in our hands. The final value of every experience depends upon its spiritual result. No one can tell what seed is in the soil until the harvest is borne ; the seed of apparent bitterness often brings forth the flowers of peace.

PAGAN WORDS

THERE are two words which ought never to be heard by children — "luck" and "chance;" the two verbal scapegoats on which are laid half the sins and follies of the race. If there is anything which is essential to the moral health and strength of a boy or girl, it is to plant deep in the consciousness the fact that this is an ordered world; that a man reaps that which he sows; that he secures the rewards for which he is willing to make the effort, and gains the prizes for which he is willing to pay the price in labor, self-denial, and strength. It is true that there are cases in which force of circumstances seem to make it impossible for a man to attain the specific end for which he sets out. In these cases, however, it is often obviously better that he should fail than that he should succeed;

for it often appears, from a later and more far-reaching point of view, that temporary failure meant ultimate success, and that in missing some one thing on which a man had set his heart he finally gained something of far greater value. What is certain in this uncertain world is that no real success is ever achieved by accident, chance, or luck; that is to say, by a blind and brutal play of forces or influences, or by a meaningless combination of conditions. What appears to be a wanton interference with human plans by a play of blind force is often seen, in the larger circuit of time, to have been the introduction of a new and higher purpose. Athens lost the political independence upon the preservation of which the greatest of her orators had set his heart, but in parting with formal independence she became sharer in a movement which spread her spirit to the ends of the earth.

In all those cases, therefore, in which on first appearance it would seem as if a man's fate had been taken out of his hands, or his dearest purposes defeated, it is well to postpone judgment until the full evolution of the movement is seen. In any case, it is the height of folly to instil into the mind the idea that a man is the play of chance winds of destiny and not the master of his own fortune. Spiritually, at least, every man shapes his own life. The things which come to him are the things for which he has prepared himself; the things which he misses are the things which he has voluntarily rejected. If he fails, it is because he lacks ability, force, skill, or judgment for the specific thing which he set out to do; if he succeeds, it is because he has the quality which commands success. If he is a man who has taught himself to be honest with himself, he never for a moment loses sight of his own fundamental responsibility. He does not permit himself the delusion that life has cheated him; that he has failed because conditions were adverse, or because some one else did not give him the support which he ought to have had. The men who are always making excuses for themselves, and laying upon others the responsibility for their own blunders, follies, and failures are rarely honest; they either deceive themselves or they evade a full, clear recognition of the facts. The beginning of education is the acceptance of the law that a man reaps what he sows, that he is responsible for his own career, and that it is idle to attempt to blind one's eyes to these fundamental facts or to shift the responsibility of one's failures to other people's shoulders.

THE LESSON OF LIFE

THE fundamental problem of life for every man and woman born into the world is very simple : it is to harmonize our wills with the will of God. The problem is simple, but the method of working it out is perplexing, painful, often agonizing. In order to do the will of God we must first find out what that will is, and this is a task which is sometimes so difficult that men give it up in despair. In the very earnestness with which they strive to know where God would lead them and what he would have them do they often bring their wills into conformity with his will without being conscious that what they sought has been found.

This is the real problem in all departments of life. In society a man must bring his desires and purposes into some kind of harmony with the rights and pleasures of all other men. In the State a man must conform his methods and his aims to the methods and aims which have been incorporated into law and political organization : if he does not do this, he becomes a law-breaker, a criminal, and an outcast. The great tragedies are the stories of men and women who have opposed their individual wills to the will of the State and have been crushed in the unequal combat. In those cases in which the State is organized or conducted in opposition to those laws of righteousness which are the expressed will of God, the State itself becomes the victim of the wilful or ignorant assertion of its own will. In the church a man conforms to the conditions under which all common religious effort must be organized and all common worship held. If men were to assert their own will in all the non-essential as well as in all the essential points of doctrine and worship, there would be as many sects as there are persons, and a church of any kind would be impossible. In the family the individual preference, desire, and ambition must be harmonized, or the beauty and sanctity of the home are ruthlessly and often brutally destroyed. It is the assertion of raw, crude, selfish individuality which wrecks so many families, breeds the scandal of easy and frequent divorce, and fills the newspapers with vulgar stories of infidelity, recrimination, and separation.

These tragedies of public, religious, and family life have their roots in the refusal of men to conform to the will of God and learn the lessons which he has set the family, the Church, and the State to teach. It is only the ignorant man who believes that freedom is to be found in self-assertion, that happiness lies in having one's way in the face of law, that the individual will can prevail against the will of the Infinite. He who has learned the elementary lessons of life has discovered that it is sheer madness to run amuck through the manifold and divinely ordered laws with which life is encompassed and by which it is protected. History presents many such figures, running with flaming torch or drawn sword through the crowded highways of society, inflicting dangerous wounds and destroying things of priceless value which lie in their paths, but doomed from the beginning to final and disastrous failure. This universe is not a chaos; although there is freedom of choice in it, no man breaks its laws and escapes the penalty. A man may wreck himself if he will; he cannot wreck God.

To refuse to conform to the law and order of the world is a sign, therefore, not of strength but of ignorance. The violent oppose, resist, storm, and hurl themselves to death against impassable barriers; the strong study, observe, learn, and accept. The violent, mistaking lawlessness for freedom, rush on

to useless and barren death; the strong,
by submission to a greater wisdom,
pass through obedience to liberty. The
strongest and most victorious figure in
history is Christ; but among all men
who have lived none ever so completely
submitted his will to the will of the
Father. In submission and resistance
lie the fortunes and fates of men. The
egotists — the raw, crude natures who
refuse to be educated — struggle, harden
themselves, persist in opposition, refuse
to be led, and are either crushed by the
tremendous forces against which they
oppose their puny strength, or are left
sterile, non-productive, bitter, and un-
comprehending — solitary figures in a
world in which men are happy and
free only in fellowship. The wise bear
the burdens, perform the tasks, submit
to the sorrows of life, because they
believe that there is a wisdom above
their own, and that that wisdom is not
only knowledge but love. They wait
upon God in order that they may learn

what he would have them do; and they
are taught by all the happenings of life,
fertilized rather than embittered by its
sorrows, and gradually led into the possession of freedom and power.

TRUE SELF-CONFIDENCE

THERE is something pathetic in the inability which prevents a great many men from believing in the best that is in them. There seems to be, if not an active, at least a passive, consciousness of infirmity and weakness which brings with it, for most men, not only spiritual modesty, but a self-distrust which stands in the way of their highest growth. This consciousness of weakness and infirmity is, in its place, one of the signs of the kinship of the human race with God; for the sense of imperfection always carries with it the conception of perfection. No man can realize how far he falls short of the mark unless he sees the mark clearly. Deep in the heart of the human race there is a profound belief in the higher possibilities of its spiritual development, and this belief is evidenced by the shrinking which prevents a great many men from taking that faith to themselves. This diffidence or self-distrust, however valuable as an element of growth, if it becomes dominant, is destructive of the power of growth. Faith may be accompanied by great consciousness of weakness, but it ought to bear its fruit in unlimited belief in the power to overcome weakness. Hosts of people miss the best things in life because they do not sufficiently strive for them. They believe abstractly in the possibility of obtaining them, but they do not believe that they are individually capable of achieving these best things; they see the stars clearly, but through self-distrust they are unable to follow Emerson's maxim and hitch their wagons to these shining points. This is not the mood of those who think or feel or do great things. Men rise above themselves — that is to say, become inspired — by putting aside their weakness and trusting to their strength, verifying those noble lines of Lowell:

True Self-Confidence

Those love truth best who to themselves are true,
And what they dare to dream of, dare to do.

As the earth is a great battery of force
which men are just learning how to use,
and which is to add immeasurably to
the working power of the world as it
becomes utilized, so the universe is
filled with tides of spiritual vitality,
upon which men can draw, and will draw,
when they come to believe in and realize
that these sources of strength are open to
them. If humanity, as a whole, would
believe practically in its ability to live
the highest life and to do the greatest
things to-morrow, society would be re-
generated, and there would come an age
of creativeness the like of which the
world has never known. For creativeness is largely a matter of attitude. God
comes to those who wait; great thoughts
are in the air for those who are open-
minded; noble impulses crowd the highways for those who are ready to receive
and act upon them. Life is commonplace very largely because men do not

put themselves in the way of becoming poets and creators. They are willing to remain mechanical when they might have the spirit and the soul of the artist ; they are content to imitate when they might fashion their own souls with their own hands. Not all men can be great, but every man can enter into the atmosphere of greatness and gain its vision ; it is simply a question of believing in the best things and in our power to attain them.

UNUSED POWER

ONE of the most interesting things in life is the unexpected development of power which sometimes takes place in people who have before shown little or no promise of exceptional energy or ability. This development is sometimes as great a surprise to the man in whom it takes place as to his friends. He awakes to find himself in possession of a force the presence of which, even in the germ, he did not suspect. What happens in such a case is not the sudden appearance in a man's nature of something which was not there before; it is the sudden disclosure of something which has hitherto been concealed. Men do not begin life fully developed. Occasionally a man appears who is as mature at twenty-five as at sixty, but this rarely happens, and when it does happen it is a distinct limitation. Young men, as a rule, are bundles of undeveloped possibilities. They grow by putting forth their strength ; and the fulness and symmetry of their unfolding depend largely upon the completeness with which they give out what is in them. When a man suddenly discloses a power the presence of which he did not suspect, he is simply putting forth what was always in him. He has created nothing new, he has taken nothing in from without ; he has simply used his own.

It is probably true that the great majority of men never fully realize their own powers, because they never completely put them forth. Society is full of undeveloped, or partially developed personalities, — men who have possibilities to which they have not given full expression, powers which they have not thoroughly trained, capacities which they have not adequately recognized. It is true that some men overwork ; that is to say, they do one thing too continuously, or they do many things without adequate refreshment and variety ; but very few men work at the top of their power. Very few men completely unfold all that is in them. As the earth is full of treasures of all kinds, the existence of which is not suspected in many localities, and which are presently to bring private fortunes and general prosperity to those localities, so there are men and women the world over who are rich in power of the highest kind, but who have no suspicion of the fact because they have never given themselves full development through activity. More men and women fail by reason of under-estimation of their power than by reason of over-valuation. As a rule, people of conscience do not take themselves at an adequate valuation ; they do not believe enough in themselves. If they believed more in their own resources, they would make more out of their lives. It is astonishing how outward circumstances will sometimes evolve unsuspected energy from a man who has heretofore been regarded as essentially

5

commonplace by his neighbors and by himself. When such a man feels the pressure of conditions, he often awakes to the possession of a power which responds quickly and adequately to a call from without. Every great crisis calls, and does not call in vain, for energy, self-sacrifice, and genius; but these things ought to come to light by virtue of inward impulse; they ought not to depend on outward conditions. A man ought to put forth all that is in him as a matter of loyalty to himself and of consecration to his fellows. He ought to lead in the evolution of spiritual energy rather than allow himself to be dependent on some bugle-call from without. To believe in ourselves in the sense of regarding ourselves as full of the germs of growth is not only to secure the highest growth, but it is to render the finest service which a man can render to his fellows.

THE POSITIVE LIFE

THERE are two general lines of action in dealing with life, the negative and the positive. A great many people approach the experiences of life and its opportunities from the negative side and are fairly successful; though the great majority of them fail to achieve any distinct character or make any lasting mark. To approach life from the negative side is to wait on opportunity, to take what the day brings, to adjust ourselves with constant self-repression to the opinions and wishes of others, to fall in with the movement of events, and to get the impetus which comes from the current. Many attain a certain kind of external success along this line. They have many well-wishers, if few warm friends; they are often popular, even if they are not greatly respected; they are sought after even when they are not honored, and the external appearance of success conceals to a certain extent the fact of failure. To this class belong all the merely politic opportunists; those who are made by conditions and advanced by circumstances, who are lifted on general movements and carried into port by fair winds. To this class belonged Lord Godolphin, of whom Charles II. once said, with characteristic wit, that he was " never in the way and never out of it."

This kind of living involves constant watchfulness of others and intense studiousness of conditions. The man who has neither steam nor sails must watch the currents very closely and keep his eye constantly on the tides. The wear and tear of constant adjustment to the wishes of the community and to fortunate conditions are never relaxed in the case of the opportunist. He can never afford to make mistakes of judgment: his success depends upon doing the politic thing at the right moment, saying the persuasive word at the proper point, and putting himself in the way at the exact second when he may be noticed or needed. He who studies popular favor in public life must needs have a quick eye and a long memory ; he must cultivate agility of motion, rapidity of thought, and skill in transferring his principles from side to side without too obvious inconsistency. This life, which seems easier, is much the hardest, because it lacks entirely that repose which comes from resting on principle, and that constant nourishment of the inward spirit which flows from harmony with the deeper laws of life.

Dealing with the positive side of life, on the other hand, involves a certain indifference to the conditions of the moment ; the indifference, not of contempt, but of preoccupation with higher things ; a certain lack of care for the opinions of others, not from selfishness or coldness, but because one's opinions are formed on a different basis. The man who actively

and positively fashions his own career
and develops his own character has an
inward purpose, an unseen aim, to which
he constantly directs his attention. He
may be a long time in forming this purpose or in perfectly discerning this aim,
but when these ultimate ends are once
clear to him he is forever rid of all uncertainty. Winds and storms are in a
certain sense matters of as little consequence to him as to the great ocean
steamers which sail to their havens with
sublime disregard of all external circumstances; they are set to a course, and
nothing drives them out of that course.
In like manner he who shapes his course
to a distant and clearly defined point is
not swept out of it by passing winds of
popular favor or disfavor, or by changing currents of popular opinion. Having an inward purpose, his relations with
men form themselves on a natural and
spiritual basis. He does not need to
weigh men according to their value for
his own uses; he is not looking to them

for the development of his own career. What he wants from them are the things which he is willing to give them — affection, sympathy, interest, and co-operation. He is not bent upon using them simply as aids; they do not work into his plan of life. He is lifted above all those sordid and selfish relationships in which a man entangles himself when he attempts to use friends to forward his own ends.

Nor need the man of inward purpose concern himself with consistency of life. There is nothing more beautiful than the reaction of a high ideal upon the actions of the man or woman who cherishes it; for an ideal steadily pursued sooner or later shapes a constant and harmonious character, and we come at last to know what the ideals of men are by the character which those ideals have formed. Nothing is so fundamental in creating a real and noble personality as the choice of a high ideal; let a man choose such an ideal and follow it loyally and he may

give up all concern for his character; it
will form itself. Such a man is emancipated, not only from the temptation to
be selfish in his friendship, but from
most of the fears that beset men of less
clearness of purpose. Such a man is
much less affected by the happenings of
outward fortune, by material disaster of
every kind, than a man who has not this
inward guidance and constant pressure
of the ideal upon his own nature. He
is emancipated from fear of men because
men can neither make nor mar his
career; he is emancipated from fear of
disaster because conditions can neither
make nor mar his career; his only
source of fear is disloyalty to his own
purpose, and that is a fear which guards
and protects rather than depresses.
Such a man discards, one by one, all
those things which belittle human life
and fill it with weakening and corroding
anxieties. He is not disturbed by the
confusion of aims which he finds in the
world about him; he is not concerned

about his enemies, for he has none whom
he has consciously made ; he thinks generously and fearlessly of his friends, and
he is lifted above all the outward changes
of fortune by the spirituality of the end
which he has chosen.

WHICH BACKGROUND?

IN the work of an artistic temperament it is easy to discover the background against which that work is done, because the background of the life of a sensitive man leaves its impress upon his imagination. Wordsworth's poetry is touched throughout with the elusive and mysterious beauty of the Lake region, and Scott's verse with the loveliness of that wild and beautiful scenery which he knew so well along the banks of the Tweed and among the southern Scottish lakes; again and again one hears in Tennyson's verse the roar of the sea along the coast of Lincolnshire, and one sees in the background of many of Titian's pictures those mountain forms with which his youth was familiar. Ruskin has described in one of his most eloquent passages the loveliness of sky and sea which enveloped the young imagination of Giorgione and gave his work its penetrating splendor.

It is not within the power of every man to choose his background. Some men are born far from the majesty of mountains and the glory of the sea. It is impossible for some men to select their surroundings; but there is another background than that of material forms, as there is another expression of a man's spirit than that of tangible work: there is a background of thought and there is a life of the mind. Those who have spiritual or literary insight are able to discern in a man's thought the background of his spiritual life; they know, if they have penetration, what images and ideals he sees in the hours when his mind is free and he lives in himself rather than in the expression of himself. One knows without being told what ideas were in the mind of Emerson when he gave free rein to his thought, and it is not difficult to imagine what kind of images thrilled Carlyle in those lonely walks in the days when "Sartor Resartus" was being written. Great spirits dwell habitually with great ideas; these ideas are their chosen companions, the intimate friends of leisure hours; it is by contact with such ideas that the springs of inspiration are fed when they have been drawn upon; it is in the fellowship of such ideas that the ideals of life are purified when they have been tarnished. The deepest and richest part of a man's life is unconscious. A great deal of his most fruitful thinking goes on without his direction, and when he is not aware that his mind is at work. The greatness of his nature and the value of his thought will depend largely upon what the mind does when he is not consciously directing it; will depend, in other words, on the ideas, the fundamental principles, the absorbing problems to which it reverts by instinct, by habit, and by affinity when it is free to select its own objects. These are its background. No man can conceal himself; no man can hide the background

Which Background?

of his mind, and that background is of his own choosing. It lies in the power of each of us to live with the greatest ideas, the noblest ideals, the most inspiring achievements in the history of man, or to content ourselves with the mediocrities, the commonplaces, and the vulgarities of our time.

THE PRAYER OF LOVE

THERE is a beautiful and significant phrase in one of the Maxims of Ani which is as full of meaning as it was when it was written, probably thirty-five hundred years ago. "What the sanctuary of God detests," wrote the wise Egyptian, "are noisy feasts; if thou implorest Him with a loving heart, . . . He will do thy affairs." There are as many forms of prayer as there are petitioners, and every form which is a natural and sincere expression of the love, the gratitude, the praise, the worship, or the need of a human spirit is good and acceptable. Men not only pray in as many languages as they speak, but every man prays in a language of his own; and God understands them all. For men use speech because they know so little of one another and must put thought or

feeling into words if they would make
either comprehensible; but God understands all before we speak, and our unuttered prayers are as audible to him as
those which we put into words.

Indeed, the value of the spoken prayer
depends entirely on the prayer which
rises to God without passing through
the mist of words; the prayer which
rises out of the deeps of our own natures,
and which is the only true and complete
expression of our spirits. Words are
idle unless there is a thought which fills
them to their full capacity. Nothing is
so valueless as speech which has no roots
in character; nothing more noble than
great speech when it is the unforced
utterance of a great faith, a great conviction, or a great purpose. Spoken
prayer is not only profitless but profane
when it is touched with perfunctoriness,
indifference, or formalism; it is unspeakably holy when it is to the silent petition
of the whole nature and life what the
few drops flung from the river into the

sunlight and shining there a brief moment are to the deep and quiet stream from which they are taken.

Every life is an invocation to the best or the worst; an invitation to good or to evil; a petition to God for forgiveness and help or an unuttered profanity. The more pure and beautiful the nature, the more sincere and noble the unspoken appeal which it makes. Every person of any sensitiveness has often felt this silent invocation of a rare and beautiful spirit. There are little children whose innocence touches us with such compassionateness that we long to take them in our arms and bear them beyond the reach of harm and pollution; there are women of such fineness of character, such exquisite harmony of nature, that we are filled with a passionate longing to shield them from care and calamity; there are generous and noble-hearted men for whom we long to clear the way, that all their rich possibilities may be brought to beautiful fruition. A fine, high, aspiring nature always makes an appeal to us, utters an unspoken prayer of which it is unconscious but which is a complete expression and revelation of its secret hopes and loves.

If these silent appeals come to us as the fragrance steals from the flower by the diffusive quality of its own sweetness, how much more direct and powerful must be their appeal to One whose history, so far as it is written in human records, is the history of a love which seeks the lost before the lost know that they are lost, and gives its life before the need of that divine sacrifice is felt? And what appeal can reach the Infinite Love so swiftly as the prayer of a loving heart; the unconscious and unspoken longing of those who love for a return of that which they are always giving? For God is not afar off; he is nearer to us than those whose voices we hear and whose hands we touch. The pure and loving are always in his presence; they do not need to speak; he understands without words; he knows all things, but he must know best the hearts that love, for they are nearest him, not only in place, but in nature. Between him and them there is a fellowship which is deeper and greater than speech; a fellowship which rests on foundations that are deeper than human consciousness. He has been always coming to them, and they are always drawing nearer to him. The prayer of a loving heart is a prayer which is granted before it is spoken; for God is love, and love goes to its own by a divine impulsion. The prayers of those that love, like the fragrance of the flowers, are the deep breathings of the soul, and the answering love of God is the atmosphere in which they exhale. The secret of prayer is not insistence; it is sharing the divine nature. They who love pray unceasingly, and unceasingly God answers them.

PERSONAL ATMOSPHERE

IN this country emphasis is continually laid upon action, as if action were the only expression of character. Now, action is in the last degree important, because character cannot be formed without it. It is through action that strength comes ; it is by action that the inchoate possibilities of a nature are rounded, harmonized, and solidified into a harmonious and developed individuality. But every action must have its reaction upon the nature of the man who puts it forth ; if it does not, it fails of that which is, for him, its highest result ; for the finest expression of a man's nature is not to be found in his action, but in that very intangible thing which we call his atmosphere. There are a great many people who are alert, energetic, and decisive, but who give forth very little of this rare and spiritual effluence — this quality which seems to issue out of the very recesses of one's nature. It is, however, through this quality that the most constant influence is exercised; that influence which is not only put forth most steadily, but which penetrates and affects others in the most searching way. The air we breathe has much to do with health; in a relaxing atmosphere it is difficult to work; in an atmosphere of vitality it is easy to work. Men are stimulated or depressed by the air they breathe; in like manner, and as unconsciously, we are stimulated or depressed by the atmosphere which envelops those with whom we associate. We never meet some men without going away from them with our ideals a little blurred or our faith in them a little disturbed; we can never part from others without a sense of increased hope. There are men who invigorate us by simple contact; something escapes from them of which they are not aware, and which we cannot analyze, which makes us believe more deeply in ourselves and our kind.

Personal Atmosphere

So far as charm is concerned, there is no quality which contributes so much to it as the subtle thing we call atmosphere. There are some women who do not need to speak in order not only to awaken our respect, but to give us a sense of something rare and fine. In such an influence all that is most individual and characteristic flows together, and the woman reveals herself without being conscious that she is making herself known. Such an atmosphere in a home creates a sentiment and organizes a life which would not be possible if one should attempt to fashion these things by intention. The finest things, like happiness, must be sought by indirection, and are the results of character rather than objects of immediate pursuit.

A man may be always less or greater than his surroundings. The key of the play for the imagination is not the stage setting, but the actor ; the audience which saw the first rendering of " Lear " or " Hamlet," with their bare surroundings and their lack of scenic effects, may have been far more profoundly stirred than many modern audiences which are assailed through every sense, but whose imagination is often entirely untouched. Nothing really moves us until a man speaks, and then we are on fire. This is what Emerson meant when he said, " The day is always his who works in it with serenity and great aims." Men are in society, not to accept things as they find them and to conform to the standards of those about them, but to create and impress their own standards ; to carry their own atmosphere with them. It is amazing how quickly any kind of original expression is recognized, and how easily the courageous man separates himself from the standards of those about him. The weary audience which has been lulled to sleep by means of a stream of commonplace talk is instantly erect and attentive when a man who has something to say, and knows how to say it, begins to speak. Such a man changes the atmosphere before his auditors are aware. He carries with him an atmosphere which silently diffuses itself. Such an atmosphere is not to be sought directly; it is to be secured only by cleansing and deepening the springs of life in the soul.

THE LARGER RELATIONSHIP

THERE is a passage in "The Mill on the Floss" which will bear meditation. "Maggie's heart," writes George Eliot, "went out toward this woman whom she had never liked, and she kissed her silently. It was the first sign within the poor child of that new sense which is the gift of sorrow — that susceptibility to the bare phases of humanity which raises them into a bond of living fellowship, as to haggard men among the icebergs the mere presence of an ordinary comrade stirs the deep fountain of affection." Behind all personal relationships which men establish with one another, there is the common bond of the universal human relationship, — this larger fellowship inclosing all lesser fellowships, as the nation includes all shades of citizenship. All men and

The Larger Relationship

women of any sensitiveness put the highest value on personal relationships, and count their friends among the foremost gifts of life and their friendships among their invaluable possessions ; but there are a great many who never recognize in any practical way the larger fellowship of humanity ; who treat friendship as if it were a luxury to be prized and guarded like a precious vase or a rare book, and not a large, free, noble opportunity for drawing out the best from another and giving the best in return.

Our friendships are often selfish without our being conscious of the fact. We look to friendship as a fountain from which only sweet waters ought to flow, — as a tie which ought to bring us only cheer, comfort, and pleasure. But friendship has obligations and duties, and is to be sought, not only among those who are by nature akin to us, and who therefore fall in with every mood and respond to every emotion, but among those who in many ways may be personally distasteful. Most men and women are thrown to a considerable degree with those to whom they are not personally drawn ; whose personality, manners, temper, or quality of mind repels rather than attracts ; and when intimacy with such persons is forced upon us by circumstances, we rebel against it as an intrusion upon a domain over which we have absolute sovereignty. Such persons often stand related to us in positions in which it is practically impossible not to accept them as friends. Our instinct tells us that we have a right to avoid intimacies with all who are not thoroughly congenial, but the conditions of life often contravene the instincts and place us in intimacies without our will.

Under these circumstances it is possible to take one of two attitudes : an attitude of unwilling acceptance, or an attitude of open-minded endeavor to get the best out of an association which we did not seek ; to attempt to substitute

for the personal tie the universal tie,
and to treat our forced companionship
as a chance to learn something more of
our common humanity. If one has the
clearness of sight and the courtesy of
soul to accept an enforced relationship
in this spirit, it is surprising how much
he can give and how much he can get
out of that relationship. Out of such
companionships, unsought and reluc-
tantly accepted, have sometimes come
the sweetest of friendships; and in all
such companionships there are the richest possibilities of mutual helpfulness
and therefore of common growth. We
cannot afford to be selfish in the selection
of our friends; if we are, we diminish
our own capacity and contract our own resources for spiritual growth. The strong
nature can afford to give where it does
not look for a return; to develop an
interest where it does not instinctively
feel one; to foster a regard and admiration when these things do not come
of themselves. It owes, as a matter of

fact, quite as much to the larger relationship which is forced upon men by the
mere fact of race-fellowship as it owes
to those carefully sought and piously
guarded relationships between man and
man which count for so much in the
joys and sorrows of life.

IN REMEMBRANCE

THERE is something very beautiful and significant in the revelation of character which death makes. On the face of one who has fallen asleep after the work of life there often comes a deep and tender peace; as if, at last, the real nature had a chance to disclose itself in the shining of the face. And those who look at the still countenance are often penetrated with the feeling that something foreign and temporary has vanished and, like the taking away of a veil, made room for that which was real and permanent. The best men and women are so involved in a multitude of small duties that they sometimes lose sight of the goal to which they are loyally moving; they are often misrepresented by personal peculiarities and passing moods, and we fail to discern each instant the large nobility of their aims. Working in crowded ranks, in the dust, heat, and uproar of the workshop of life, we fail to recognize the greatness or beauty of those who stand beside us. But when death comes and brings its wonderful silence, all the mists and clouds vanish, and we see with clear vision. Then, in an instant, the long patience, the high idealism, the hatred of meanness, the passionate pursuit of the best, the affection which was tenderly urgent rather than weakly indulgent, shine before us, and we wonder that our eyes were so long holden. And as the years go by and the perspective of time lengthens, the true proportions of character, the large lines of life, become more distinct. Blessed are the dead when they live with increasing nobility and beauty in the memory of those who knew and loved them!

Recognition is a matter of secondary importance to the brave, the true, and the good; but it is a matter of prime importance to others. Not to discern nobility in every form, or to suffer it to become obscured by personal peculiarities or moods, is to miss one of the richest opportunities of growth. It is well to remember that only the good believe in the good, and to the noble alone is given the power to recognize that which is noble.

"It is a true discrimination," said Phillips Brooks, "that recognizes the presence of God in men, the saints that are in the world, not by the miracles they work but by the miracles they are, by the way in which they bring the grace of God to bear on the simple duties of the household and the street. The sainthoods of the fireside and of the market-place — they wear no glory round their heads; they do their duties in the strength of God; they have their martyrdoms and win their palms, and though they get into no calendars, they leave a benediction and a force behind them on the earth when they go up to heaven."

THE CONTAGION OF FAITH

IT is a significant fact that every intelligent man finds it necessary to have what is called a working theory of life; in other words, every man feels compelled, in order to live at all and do any work, to accept some conception of life which makes room for action and place for hope. The consistent pessimists who believe nothing and hope for nothing are few. In pessimism there are almost numberless gradations, from despair up to that conventional pose into which so many people have fallen of late years, — fallen so completely that it has become second nature to look at the dark side of things and to take gloomy views. This attitude does not, however, in the least interfere with the pleasure which the average pessimist finds in life, nor with the satisfaction which he takes in his own work. He has, as has been said, "the best possible time in the worst possible world." The men who profess to find neither order nor meaning nor beauty in life are very often persons who work as if the objects which they are striving to obtain were worth securing; who hold themselves to a scrupulous performance of duty, as if duty were not only obligatory, but were worth doing; and who are loyal in all their personal relations, as if loyalty were not only a matter of morality but also a source of pleasure.

To be consistently pessimistic one must believe nothing, hope nothing, and do nothing. The moment a man hopes, believes, or acts, he ceases to be a consistent pessimist. An effective argument can be made for pessimism as a philosophical theory; as a working theory it is untenable unless one so modifies it as practically to destroy its force. There are a few smitten and hunted creatures here and there in society who, if they took their own experience as a basis for a judgment of the value of life, might, with some show of decency, proclaim themselves pessimists; but, by an enormous majority, men in all parts of the world, and in the worst times, find something which is worth living for and something which is worth doing. The man who follows pessimism to a consistent end is to be found only in the list of suicides. The instincts of humanity, as well as its intelligence, its insight, and its inspiration, are against a view of life which makes life unbearable.

But while pessimism as a working theory finds very few consistent adherents, pessimism as an intellectual pose finds many who are only too ready to take courage out of the hearts of those with whom they have influence; for the most unfortunate result of the pessimistic pose is the devitalization which it effects. It takes the tonic out of the atmosphere in which men live; it saps their hopes in the exact degree in which they accept it; it not only destroys their illusions but their aspirations as well. It is a kind of blight on the finer growths of the spirit. The best things in men are evoked by their own faith in themselves, or by the faith of others in them. He who believes that another is base has taken the first step, and perhaps the most effective one, toward making that other base; while he who treats one who is undeserving as if he were deserving has taken the first and perhaps the most effective step toward rehabilitating a fallen man.

There are two spirits in every man, and these spirits are contending together for the mastery. In all our relations we make our choice whether we shall evoke the best or the worst in those whom we meet; whether we shall liberate the best that is in them or invigorate the worst. There are men who go through life and do no evil so far as action is concerned, but who blight everything fine and fair which comes in their way, by the chilling breath of skepticism; there are others who have a genius for calling out the best. It was impossible not to believe in the nobility and dignity of life when one listened to Phillips Brooks; his atmosphere made skepticism incredible. When Hume declared that he believed in immortality whenever he remembered his mother, he was bearing testimony to the almost divine influence which women of the highest type always exert, and which they often exert in entire unconsciousness. What a man believes or what he disbelieves is a vital matter, not only for himself, but for others. Let him believe in the best, and, however full of faults and imperfections he may be, there will be in his own nature a slow but tidal movement toward goodness, and he will make the attainment of virtue easier for all who know him. Let a man disbelieve in the possibility of purity, integrity, and unselfishness, and, although he may have great ability and many attractive qualities, he will smirch the society through which he passes, and leave a blackened trail behind him.

The Contagion of Faith

When a man comes to look back on his own life, his most blessed comfort may be the discernment for the first time that he has helped instead of hindered; and his most terrible punishment may be the discernment for the first time of the aid which he has given unconsciously and unintentionally to the process of moral disintegration and spiritual decline in those about him.

DANGEROUS FOES

IT was said of Jeremy Taylor that " nature had befriended much in his constitution, for he was a person of most sweet and obliging humour, and of great candour and ingenuity. . . . His soul was made up of harmony ; and he never spoke but he charmed his hearer, not only with the clearness of his reason, but all his words, and his very tone and cadences, were musical." This disclosure of a winning temper in a man of great genius finds its explanation in part in certain comments of the eloquent preacher touching what he calls little vexations : —

" . . . be careful to stifle little things," he writes, " that as fast as they spring they be cut down and trod upon ; for if they be suffered to grow by numbers, they make the spirit perish, and the society troublesome, and the affections loose and easy by an habitual aversation. Some men are more vexed with a fly than with a wound ; and when the gnats dis-

turb our sleep, and the reason is disquieted but not
perfectly awakened, it is often seen that he is fuller
of trouble than if, in the daylight of his reason, he
were to contest with a potent enemy. In the frequent little accidents of a family a man's reason cannot always be awake; and, when the discourses are
imperfect, and a trifling trouble makes him yet more
restless, he is soon betrayed to the violence of passion."

This goes to the very heart of the un-
doing of fine natures by small discom-
forts, petty annoyances, little troubles.
They lose serenity, sweetness, and dignity
because they fail to recognize the fact
that a sting may be as dangerous as a
wound, and that the trifle which costs a
man his self-respect is as important, so
far as he is concerned, as the great pro-
vocation which throws him into passion.
Character is fundamental in all relations; without it there is no real,
genuine, effective human intercourse or
co-operation. In all conditions and for
all purposes it is essential that we should
be able to trust our fellow and to secure
and hold his confidence. Next to char-

acter the most essential qualities for comfort, peace, and happiness are sweetness and serenity of spirit. These qualities are atmospheric in their nature ; they diffuse themselves through space; they make the weather in which we live ; they flood us with sunlight or blight us with chill and gloom. Cheerfulness and sweetness are commonly regarded as temperamental. In many cases they are the natural expressions of harmonious and well-balanced natures. But they are quite as often the " lovely result of forgotten toil " ; qualities which, by patience, care, and persistence, have been developed out of the most unpromising soil by refusal to yield to the tyranny of small vexations and the wear of wearisome details which of necessity fill a large place in every life.

These petty annoyances crowd every path of work or pleasure, and one must elect whether he will brush them aside with a strong hand or permit them to spring up and choke the finer growths in his soul. The irritable man is something more than a trial to the men who work with him and something worse than a steady discomfort; he is a depressor of vitality and therefore a waster of power. The warm, genial air does not invite delicate things out of the soil more potently than does the man of serene, sunny nature call forth the best energies of his co-workers. When such a man is in command, no time need be lost in attempts to make working adjustments with him; every man can put his whole force into his task. The irritable, peevish spirit in the household, succumbing to every petty annoyance, is absolutely fatal to that sweet and deep peace in which alone the affections put forth all their tendrils and bear their most delicate blossoms. There are women about whom the whole world blooms; where they are it is always June.

There is something pitiful in the defeat of a man by insignificant foes. When a strong nature falls before a powerful antagonist, there is the sense of tragedy, but there may be no sense of humiliation; but when a sting does the work of a wound, there comes a certain feeling of contempt. In the battle of life, which is a struggle, not only for integrity, but for sweetness, serenity, and peace, every man owes it to his fellows to make a brave fight. There is a kind of treason in surrender to petty foes. There are so many great troubles in life, so many appalling calamities, so many heavy burdens to be borne, and such difficult tasks to be performed, that it is cowardly to yield peace and sweetness to insignificant assaults on patience and good temper.

We are bound, not only to resist the things that imperil our integrity and peace, but to aid and succor our fellows. The man who flies into a passion because some small thing goes wrong, who is peevish, irritable, and disagreeable when additional work comes unexpectedly or unforeseen accidents occur, not only makes life harder for every one about him, but makes it harder at the very time when it is his plain duty to make it easier. The moral of the whole matter is that there are no small things; that the annoyance, however apparently insignificant, which costs a man his temper, is really important; and that we owe our fellows the duty of sweetness and cheerfulness quite as much as the duty of fidelity and honesty. On the eve of Agincourt, the quiet hopefulness of Henry V. was worth another army to the decimated English. In the ebb and flow of the daily struggle of men in the work of the world, the cheerful and sunny are bringers of strength and harbingers of victory.

INVITING THE BEST THINGS

THE house which has been deco-
rated and furnished out of hand by
an expert holds a relation to its owner
very different from that which is held by
a house which represents his individual
taste and has been gradually conformed
in color and form to his individuality.
The house which the expert prepares as
a matter of skill is often very beautiful,
but it never has the significance possessed by the house which discloses
everywhere the touch of a single personality slowly evolving an outward
harmony in response to an inward
craving for order and beauty. It is
wise to have beautiful things about us,
even if we do not comprehend or enjoy
them ; but it is far wiser to surround
ourselves with harmonious colors and
forms because we cannot rest content in
any kind of discord.

Inviting the Best Things

True preparation for orderly, beautiful, and dignified ways of living must be made within a man; and the visible beauty with which he surrounds himself ought to be a key to his tastes. There is an attractive power in character which we rarely understand, but which is the key to outward prosperity of all kinds. The happenings of life lie in wait along the highway until the person to whom they belong by natural affiliation appears, and then instantly attach themselves to him. To the passionate, lawless, and violent, things of kindred nature are always hastening with swift, unerring feet. For him who takes the sword the sword is always in readiness. The fates are asleep until we awaken them; they never come unsought; they await our invitation, and are powerless until we open the doors to them. The witches on the blasted heath predicting greatness to Macbeth did not destroy a noble nature. Banquo heard the same fateful words, but the doors of his spirit were

locked and bolted by loyalty and integrity, and over him the spirits of evil
had no power. Macbeth had long been
making ready for them, and their words
of fate fell into a quick soil. All his life
the future murderer and tyrant had been
inviting the day when, in the storm of
battle, his own life should be extinguished
as mercilessly as he had put out the light
of countless other lives.

To men and women of unbalanced
ambitions, unrestrained passions, un-
controlled temper, tragedy is always
approaching. They are marked for
disaster, not by a fate outside themselves, but by the very structure of
their own nature. Violence is sown for
the violent as light is sown for the
righteous; in the end every man faces
himself in the harvest he has to reap,
and no man reaps what he has not sown.

The unselfish and loving, who serve
and wait, are often astonished by the
affection and devotion they evoke. They
cannot understand how so much has

come to them when they feel so keenly their own poverty of spirit and are filled with a deep and genuine self-dissatisfaction. They are always sowing the seeds of kindness, but when their ways blossom with all manner of beautiful words and deeds, they do not recognize the fruit of their own sweetness and devotion. They are always inviting kindness, affection, and trust, and these qualities are always lying in wait along their paths in a thousand beautiful forms.

If one longs for a noble and harmonious life, with the resources of taste, intelligence, and culture, with the warmth which comes into the air of the world from troops of friends, with such an external ordering of life in estate, house, furnishings, and social order as shall express a high-minded and generous spirit, let him prepare his own character for these great prosperities. To the man of harmonious nature, fine taste, and kindly spirit, the things which give external life order, beauty, and dignity are always coming. If one sets out to acquire these things and add them to himself, they generally evade and escape him ; they are not waiting for him; and when he comes they do not know him. But let him be in his own spirit what he desires to express in his belongings, and all these things shall be added to him ; they belong to him, and, as a rule, they are waiting for him.

THE GRACE OF GOODNESS

THERE is a tact of the spirit which,
by a deep instinct, divines that
which will hurt and that which will heal
in human intercourse. This is the fine
grace of those saints who stay in the
world without a touch of worldliness,
who live with as much purity as the
strictest ascetic, but who shed the radiance of their devotion along the highway
of life instead of prisoning it in a cell;
who have many interests but never waste
or dissipate spiritual energy; and who
make men aware of the reality of the
highest ideals without so much as hint-
ing that they exist.

Honesty is one of the foundation
stones of character, but honor is finer
than honesty, because it transforms honesty into a spiritual quality by lifting
it above all considerations of policy or
advantage. A man may be honest and

yet grasping and small; but the man who has a delicate sense of honor adds to integrity the grace of unselfishness. Goodness is always admirable, but there are degrees of goodness, as there are degrees of culture. It is a great deal, amid the manifold temptations of life, to find the immovable foundations and build upon them; but all builders do not have the same feeling for harmony of mass and line, for sound and beautiful construction. Ugly houses are sometimes reared on foundations massive enough to support a palace or a cathedral. The flowers and fragrance of goodness are often lacking in those who possess its roots. They are honest, truthful, faithful to all trusts and duties; but they do not diffuse the sweetness of faith in the very best things; they are not enveloped in the atmosphere which evokes from others all the finer qualities and reinforces all their higher convictions.

The good are not always winning; they do not always commend the influences that shape them by their manifestation of those influences. They command confidence, but they do not make converts. Such men and women do much of the necessary work of the world; they carry its burdens with silent heroism; they are often of the stuff of which saints are made, but they have not attained sainthood. They lack the higher harmony which comes to those who so completely forget themselves that the whole nature silently conforms itself to the will of God.

The gentleness and tenderness of Christ were expressed in a consideration for others, based on a perception of their needs, sorrows, and imperfections, which makes him the first gentleman in the world as well as its most radical reformer. Appointed to do the most destructive work as a means of reorganizing society on a truer foundation, he carried on his warfare with weapons which healed as they smote; hating the sin of the world with all the intensity of a sinless nature, he, above all men whose words and deeds have been recorded, loved more than he condemned and saved in the exact measure in which he destroyed.

This spiritual sensitiveness to the needs of others breeds the divine tact which makes the touch of the uncanonized saints so gentle and healing. They move among the sick, the weary, the sinful, with a quiet helpfulness which is a kind of health in itself. Instead of breaking and bruising, they bind up and heal. A deep compassion flows from them and envelops in an atmosphere of sympathy those whom they would help. They refresh us before we understand how weary we are; they make us aware of our shortcomings in our innermost hearts and ashamed in our very souls without so much as intimating that they see any fault in us.

Many men and women, with the best intentions in the world, go blundering through life, hurting where they would heal and giving pain where they would bring peace, simply from dulness of spiritual perception. The pathetic prayer which Mr. Sill puts into the mouth of the Fool, and which sinks into the heart of the King, ought to be oftener on our lips:

" The ill-timed truth we might have kept—
    Who knows how sharp it pierced and stung?
The word we had not sense to say —
    Who knows how grandly it had rung?

" Our faults no tenderness should ask,
    The chastening stripes must cleanse them all;
But for our blunders — oh, in shame
    Before the eyes of heaven we fall ! "

The blunders of the good are sometimes more difficult to repair than evil deeds; and they are few against whom these lost or ill-used opportunities cannot be charged.

Most of us are in the rudimentary stages of spiritual growth; we lack the sensitiveness of spirit which makes the saints ministering angels; we are shut out, by our lack of insight, from that finer service which is possible only to those who look into the hearts of their fellows, and through this knowledge turn their love into a healing wisdom.

PERSONAL DEFLECTION

A LITTLE collection of aphorisms, recently printed but not published, contains, among other pieces of practical wisdom and spiritual insight, this bit of advice: "Protect your compass from personal deflection." The protection of the compass so as to preserve the navigator from the consequences of deflection is a matter of prime importance. So much study has been devoted to this end that the caring for the compass has become a matter of science. A great many people do not understand that the compass which every man carries in his own mind is in danger of constant shiftings from the pole by reason of his own temperament, habits, and personal experience. The judgment of a great many people is constantly vitiated by the fact that it is based largely, not on a broad observation of facts, but on personal feelings, and on the reactionary effects of personal experience. Half the pessimism to which men give expression in terms of general condemnation of things as they are arises from personal failure or disappointment. The man who has failed in his own enterprises is always in danger of finding the reason for his failure, not in himself, but in conditions, and in arriving at wholly false conclusions in regard to those conditions. Nothing is so difficult as to keep one's self in perfectly sane and real relations to one's work, one's fellows, and to the spiritual environment of life. There are very few whose days are not often clouded; who are not hampered in working out their ideas by defects in their own temper and by the limitations of their own minds; but no man can see clearly and judge wisely who does not know these things and take them into account. When a wise man finds himself in a mood of depression, he may not be able at the instant to throw it off, but he refuses to come to decisions while he is under its spell, because he knows that his judgment is, for the time being, vitiated. There are a great many days when a wise man refuses to act, because he knows that his compass is deflected.

Perhaps the first element of success, in the largest sense of the word, is to be able to put ourselves out of account in reaching general conclusions and taking final positions. Because a man is sick, it does not follow that all society is out of joint; because a man fails, it does not mean that the industrial system is wrongly organized; because a man does not attain his personal ambition, it does not mean that he is in a heartless world surrounded by those who will not recognize ability and character. When a man begins to feel a sense of personal injury, it is time for him to take account of his own state of mind, and to ask whether he is not out of true relations to his fellows by reason of his own attitude. Against the impression which the moment gives, as

Emerson suggested, must be put the impression which comes from the year and the century; the detail must be viewed in the light of the completed whole. Individual disaster must be constantly looked at in relation to the general order of things; and one of the finest achievements of an honest man is to be able to disentangle himself from the bitterness of defeat or the anguish of sorrow, and look at the world in an impersonal and objective spirit. A good many pious and wise men of the mystical temper have sought clearness of vision by withdrawing themselves from human relationships and the entanglements of practical affairs; but the finest vision is that which a man secures when, in the midst of relationships and affairs, he is able to look at the great whole of life as if he were standing apart from it, and there were no bitter pressure from its impact on his own fortunes or his individual happiness.

THE DISCIPLINE OF SUCCESS

IT is a traditional feeling that the discipline of life comes only from things which are hard and disagreeable; the things which give pleasure are commonly regarded by those who are unthoughtful as devoid of self-denial and self-surrender. In like manner, and with kindred shortness of sight, we interpret as providential those happenings which manifestly forward our interests and plans, oblivious of the oft-taught lesson of history that apparent prosperities are often adversities of the most searching kind, and that what seems at the moment to be the worst possible fortune turns to gold in the unfolding of its hidden potency. And in like manner also, we are moved to expression of gratitude to God when fields have been white and granaries are full, while our thanksgiving shrinks into the narrowest and shallowest rivulet of praise when material conditions are adverse, even though they are actively making for the richest growth of the spirit. To those who put themselves in the way of divine guidance adversity is as truly blessed as prosperity, and narrowness of means forwards the highest interests as definitely as opulence.

The discipline of adversity has been so constantly studied and commented upon by the moralists of every age that all the world recognizes it as a reality, whether it profits by its knowledge or not; but the disciplinary side of success often escapes observation. In the golden light which surrounds an obviously prosperous career harsh outlines are so softened that they often fade out altogether. But the successful man, if he has any clear self-knowledge, knows that he is being relentlessly tested, and that the sternest adversity could not more searchingly reveal the quality of his character. The struggles of success are forgotten in the opportunities, the comfort, and the applause which come with it; but no successful man escapes its temptations. Every man of insight knows that good fortune, if it is his, is to be found, not in his prosperity, but in the spirit in which he meets and bears it. To keep the moral fibre firm, the head clear, the heart warm, the tastes simple, when the spirit is assailed on all sides by temptations to ease, to complacency, to selfishness, to luxury, involves a moral struggle which is not less severe because it is fought out under comfortable conditions. The tests of success are more searching than those of adversity because the temptations of prosperity are more subtle and insidious than those of adversity. The unsuccessful man sees the foes he is fighting; they are in the open field, and he can hardly fail to take their measure. The successful man is assailed by foes which take advantage of his ease to attack when his guard is lowered.

It was said of a man of great wealth,

who was stricken down in his early prime,
that he had died in a heroic effort to
administer a hundred million dollars con-
scientiously. People at large, when they
thought of him, thought chiefly of the
almost unlimited opportunities of enjoyment which immense wealth offered him ;
he thought chiefly of the great responsibilities which it imposed upon him. To
the world his colossal prosperity was the
symbol of pleasure ; to him it was a stern
discipline, under the pressure of which
his character took on the firmness and
vigor of a moral athlete, but his body
sank under the burden. To the thoughtless, wealth stands for ease and pleasure ;
but the vast majority of those who possess
it find it full of work and care. And this
is true of every kind of success ; the
world sees its splendor, its apparent ease,
or its opportunities of enjoying the pleasures of influence, affluence, and reputation ; the man who possesses it feels
chiefly its responsibilities and thinks
chiefly of the work it imposes upon him.

The Discipline of Success

For the successful men are the heroic toilers of our time; for them all fixed working hours are abolished; life is one great hour of toil. To a man like Mr. Gladstone work is not a matter of times and seasons; it is the absorbing necessity of a lifetime. He may not be indifferent to the satisfaction which fame carries in its hands; but he is occupied habitually with the colossal work which his position brings with it. And this is true of all men who are really successful; for success lies within a man, no matter how prosperous his conditions may be; and he only can be held successful who receives with an open mind and a willing spirit the discipline which prosperity brings as relentlessly as adversity.

THE BEST PREPARATION

THE best preparation for the future does not consist in thinking about it, nor primarily in planning for it, but in doing the work of the day with the largest intelligence and the keenest conscience. The schoolboy is not prepared for the tasks and responsibilities of manhood by continually dwelling on the things he will do when he becomes a man; it is well that he should think very little about them, and that the emphasis of his thought should rest on the work, the play, and the pleasure of the moment. He will have his dreams, as every boy of intelligence has them, and the future will beckon him on with a thousand invisible signs and a thousand inaudible voices, to which his heart and imagination will continually respond: but it is not the future on which his mind ought to dwell; it is the present. He who thinks wisely of the present and does well with the present thinks most wisely and does best with the future; for the future is but the unfolding of the present. The wise farmer spends very little time in meditating on his harvest at the time of seed-sowing; his whole concern is to get the seed under the ground under the best possible conditions, and to give it the best possible care. So far as he can control it, the future is involved in every day's work.

This is true in every relation of life. Work and action ought to be planned so far as either lies within the control of the planner; every life ought to be dominated by a general aim; every one ought to be working for some ultimate purpose; but the ultimate purpose is accomplished and the remotest goal reached, not by continually meditating upon them, but by getting the vantage-ground which comes when each day receives the deposit of all that a man can give out of his conscience, his intelligence, and his character, and every year sums up the entire capacity of his nature in what has been done. They are right who insist that we ought to cultivate the expectation of good fortune and to put out of our minds the apprehension of calamity; for we best prepare ourselves for misfortune by the serenity and poise of mind which anticipates and demands the best from life. Strength comes, not from building shelters for one's self against possible disasters, but from living bravely and freely as if there were no enemy in sight. The man who is always skulking across the field seeking some form of shelter is quite as likely to fall as the man who bravely faces the fire from the most commanding position. One man shapes his life by fear, and the other by courage; neither is secure, because in one sense there is no security in life, danger being always present; but courage is far more safe than cowardice. The best preparation for the future,

The Best Preparation

whether for work, calamity, trial, or task, is to do thoroughly, bravely, and cheerfully those things which fall to our hand day by day. It is after this fashion that the greatest works are accomplished; it is by this method that the finest characters are formed; it is in this way that the wisest train themselves for life. He who gives himself up to thoughts of heaven and anticipations of happiness denies himself that preparation for heaven which comes by accepting the education of life, and which is the only sure promise of the possession of heaven. We must create heaven within ourselves before we claim it as a condition.

FAITH-INSPIRERS

IT is the advance, whether by the movement of a whole army or the swift charge of a brigade, which carries the field and plucks the flower of victory. Prudence preserves that which is already secured; faith, courage, and enthusiasm make new conquests. There is immense force in mere momentum. An army like Alexander's derives its strength, not from fortified places left in the rear, nor from intrenched camps, but from the very swiftness of its movement. Like an avalanche it multiplies itself as it descends. It is a notable fact that all great leaders have been great faith-inspirers. They have made men believe in their genius and their fortune, and have divided with a multitude the precious gift of enthusiasm which, like a star, has led them on. Alexander inspired implicit faith, not only in himself, but in the men

who were under him. They came to regard themselves as invincible, and this
belief was one secret of their sustained
success. When men profoundly believe
that they are to succeed, success is already
won. It is the positive men who accomplish great things ; the negative men
conserve, but they do not enlarge the
borders of knowledge or of achievement.
In science, literature, and business they
keep that which has been already won,
but no new beauty, no new ideal, no new
prosperity ever comes from their hands.

The great hopes of the world spring
from the hearts of those who believe,
and who set themselves to act with the
positive forces of society. The greatest service which any man can render
to his fellows is to inspire them with faith
in themselves, to make them believe that
they are capable of the highest things, to
fill them continually with that deep confidence which springs, not from over-
estimate of self, but from a resolute hold
upon fundamental principles, an uncon-

querable faith in noble and worthy causes.
There are few things impossible to those
who believe; but most men are so surrounded by limitations, so beset by
doubts, that they distrust their own
powers and disbelieve the dreams of their
hearts. Every man who has not utterly
wrecked himself knows that he was born
for the best things. This is the hope
which life continually sets before him;
this is the presence of God forever re-
vealing itself in him. To hear this inner
voice and follow it; to make aspiration
not a dream which lies like a sunset light
on the horizon, but a quenchless star
which burns forever before one's confident feet, is to put one's self in the line
of the noblest success. There are men
and women whose whole atmosphere is
critical, skeptical, and depressing; there
are others out of whom confidence is
breathed, and from whom strength goes
forth unconsciously to themselves. They
always appeal to that which is noblest in
their fellows; they always inspire their

Faith-Inspirers

fellows with new hope and fresh courage. There is no joy in life greater than to be one of these faith-inspirers, to have this sublime health of spirit which makes the very hem of one's garment healing, and diffuses courage, hope, and faith like an atmosphere.

THE TEST OF OPPORTUNITY

THE incident of the boatload of shipwrecked men, dying of thirst, who accidentally dropped a bucket into what they supposed to be the sea, and found they were sailing in the fresh water of the mouth of the Amazon, has been used until it is threadbare ; but it is, nevertheless, a capital illustration of what is happening this very hour to a multitude of men and women. There are a host of people who suppose themselves to be eager to find their work in life and longing for an opportunity, who are surrounded by work and opportunity which they fail to recognize. The real difference between men is not in their chances, but in their ability to recognize their chances. Opportunities are universal. They come in one form or another to every human being. It is safe to say that no man lives whose hand at some time has not been at the door of a genuine opportunity, if he had only raised his eyes and discovered that his hand was no longer resting on an unbroken wall. The trouble is that we do not see. We are so intent upon having things come to us after some manner which we have determined upon in our own minds, that when they come to us in some other guise we let them pass unnoticed. The common opportunity comes, as the divinest opportunity in the whole history of the world came, cradled in obscurity.

Opportunities wear the humblest dress; they hide themselves behind the simplest disguises; there is nothing in them that arouses our interest or awakens our suspicion; for the most part we pass them by as the most commonplace things in our environment. This is the subtle and dangerous test which they apply to us. If they came with their value disclosed by the splendor of their attire, there would be no test of character in the manner in which we met them. Every man treats a king handsomely; it is only the gentleman who is courteous to the beggar. Opportunities come in such fashion that our reception of them determines our fitness to use them. The man or woman of true wisdom knows that there is nothing in this world which has not noble possibilities in it, and that appearances count for nothing when quality is concerned. It is not by accident, therefore, that some men succeed and others fail; that some men seem to be passing steadily upward and others remain hopelessly stationary. The men who succeed are open-minded; they are alert to discover the true value of things; they do not estimate the importance of events by their appearances; they take everything at its best and use it for its highest. So there lies at the bottom of every right use of opportunities a noble quality of character — that quality which takes life as a divine thing, full of noble chances of growth and progress. No one will read these words, however obscure or remote from the great centres of human activity, about whom there are not doors ready to be opened into a wider usefulness and a nobler life. What we need is, not a new chance, but clearness of vision to discern the chance which at this very hour is ours, if we recognize it.

THE STERILITY OF REST-
LESSNESS

THE wide-felt need of calmness of
nerves and mind is expressed
in many ways in these days. Some
of these ways are sane and wise; some
of them are unwholesome and misleading; but whether wise or foolish,
they are alike significant of the consciousness of the lack of something
which is necessary for the truest growth
and fruitfulness. The world is full of
restless men and women, who are vainly
seeking in some place or philosophy or
person that repose which can come only
from inward peace. The ends of the
earth are searched for that which lies
close at hand, and distant and alien
religions are invoked to bestow that
which the seeker can find only in his
own spirit. This restlessness is often

confused by its victims with intellectual
and spiritual energy, and the mere agitation of a wasted nervous force is mistaken for a genuine activity of the soul.
An immense amount of vitality is ex-
pended in simply changing localities
without changing the spirit. The multitude of invalids and semi-invalids who
are seeking health in remote climates is
matched by another multitude who are
seeking peace and repose by getting
into the atmosphere of other faiths and
traditions.

As there are world-travellers hurrying
across every sea and rushing from point
to point on every continent, so there are
soul-travellers who are never at rest, but
are constantly hurrying from philosophy
to religion and from religion back to
philosophy. And so there has grown
up a kind of polyglot knowledge which
is not and cannot become culture ; and
a polyglot religion in which there is
neither the power of personal experience
nor the peace which flows from individ-

ual conviction. It is not by searching the earth with tireless feet that men come to know their own natures, nor by worshipping at many shrines that they enter into that peace which passes knowledge. Restlessness is always the sign of a life unfulfilled and a soul unsatisfied; it is a conclusive evidence that one has not come into that harmonious relation with himself and the world which is the first step towards real growth. Agitation often accompanies a deep experience, but when the lesson of the experience has been learned the agitation gives place to peace. The first contact with a new field of work or of knowledge often moves the spirit profoundly; but when one has taken possession of the field, or put his hand resolutely to the work, calmness comes. For it is only in peace and repose that truth reveals its deeper aspects, the spirit comes to self-knowledge, and real growth begins. We do not begin to grow in power and wisdom until we strike deep roots into the soil; and he who is always travelling gets no rootage. In the old German student life the year of wandering had its recognized place as an invaluable part of education; but it was an experience of preparation, not a continuing habit. It was the path by which the learner came at last to his home; for it is only in a true home that the soul lives its normal life.

SOMETHING TO BE
CULTIVATED

THERE are few qualities which lie so directly within the reach of every man and woman, because so immediately the result of education, as self-control; and yet there are few qualities which are so generally lacking. Everybody has a certain amount of self-control, but there are many people who compensate themselves for the repression of their energies on one side by giving them full play on another. Self-control means the entire mastery of one's nature; means always having in hand all one's powers; means sitting on the box and driving, instead of being driven. The absence of self-control is seen in many small ways: in the unconscious raising of the tones of voice in earnest talking, in purely nervous gesticulation and rest-

lessness; in the inability to drop a sub-
ject when we have gotten through with
it; in irritability, and that subdued
violence, shown, not in outbursts of
temper, but in little gusts of passion,
escaping here and there. These are all
small things in themselves, but many
of them are exceedingly irritating and
disagreeable, and they all involve a loss
of nervous force. The heightened tone
of the voice, the incessant gesticulation,
the physical restlessness, are not only
unpleasant, but they involve needless
expenditure of a force of which few of
us possess a superabundance. Complete
self-control is one of the fundamental
qualities in any large and high success;
for complete self-control means that one
has one's self completely in hand, and
is able to address one's self entirely to
whatever is necessary to be done at the
moment. It is a great mistake to infer
power from any kind of violence or restlessness; true power is allied with composure, with calmness, with self-restraint;

and real power is manifested in restraint and composure, and not in violence of speech or action. A man of nervous organization recently said that he had gained immense benefit by simply watching the modulations of his voice, and persistently resisting the inclination to run into high tones. He had found not only relief for the vocal chords, but a steadiness and calmness of thought and feeling which made him conscious of the great blunder of wasting nervous strength by suffering the vocal chords to sympathize with an excited condition rather than keeping them under steady control. This is one illustration of the possibility of overcoming the common forms of nervousness. To "let one's self go" is not only to lose force at a particular point, but to invite a reaction along the whole line of physical expression, and so to continually stir up and agitate, instead of continually restraining and calming. Many people lay these minor faults on the shoulders of a nervous

146

temperament, and do not know that a nervous temperament, under control, is a tremendous force, and as susceptible of being governed by the will as the grosser appetites or passions.

THE TRIUMPHANT LIFE

THERE is nothing more inspiring than the story of a triumphant life which overcomes great difficulties, works itself clear of sharp limitations, and issues at last in a large, free activity. It is an old story, but it remains the one story of which men never tire, and which seems to assuage a thirst of the soul. For the end of life is freedom and power, and those who miss these supreme results of patience and toil and character feel that they have been defrauded of that which was their due. The old stories of magic carry a deep meaning under their wild extravagances; they betray the mighty passion of men for supremacy over things material and over inferior orders of life. The man with genii at his command could build palaces in a night, and rejoice in a marvellous mastery over the forces against which so many of his fellows seemed to measure their strength in vain. These magical successes are foreshadowings of the real successes which all men and women crave; which the noblest and most aspiring must secure, or lose the joy and sweetness of living. These real successes are not external, though they are generally accompanied by visible trophies; they are achievements of character, and are largely independent of conditions and of human recognition. The man whose life, outwardly all defeat, is steadily expanding in its interests and sympathies, steadily growing in power to bear and suffer and be strong, has the blessed consciousness of coming into his kingdom. No outward disaster, no external obstacle or limitation, can ever defeat a true life; it can escape all these things as the bird escapes the perils of the snare and the net by flying above them. This highest of all successes lies within the grasp of every earnest man and woman, and it is rarely without attestations of its presence and value, even in the eyes of those who take small account of spiritual things. There is a force which streams from a noble nature which is as irresistible and pervasive as the sunlight. The warmth and the vitality of such natures, while they invigorate the strongest men and women about them, penetrate to the heart of clouded and obscure lives, and minister to their need. There is no success so satisfying as that which is embodied in one's character, and so cannot be taken from him, and the influence of which, embodied in the character of others, is also indestructible.

THE BEST IN THE WORST

IN one of Browning's most inspiring poems there is a passage in which the poet, imagining himself face to face with death, declares that

" Sudden the worst turns the best to the brave."

This is no fanciful touch of the imagination, but a statement of a fact which has occurred again and again in innumerable lives. History is full of stories of the sudden turn of fortune when things were at their worst, and when there was apparently no possibility of anything but final disaster. That which has been true of life on a large scale has been eminently true of individual lives; in which again and again, when fortune has been at the lowest ebb, the tide has turned. It is always hardest to believe in this possibility when such a belief would bring consolation and courage. When things are going well, and the outlook is bright, it is easy to fortify one's self with philosophy, and to hold up between one's self and adversity and calamity those shields of faith and truth which others have found invulnerable in the hour of need ; but it is a different thing, when one's whole happiness or material prosperity is at stake, to face the possibilities of the future with calmness and courage. Nevertheless, these are the times when every one should take counsel with his hopes and not with his despair. It is an old proverb, which in one form or another has found its way into almost every language, that "Man's extremity is God's opportunity." When the Jew consoled himself by repeating the maxim of his nation, "In the mount God will be found," he recalled one of the sorest trials to which a human soul was ever subjected, and one of the most despairing situations in which such a soul was ever placed. To those who fight the battle courageously there often comes, at the very moment when everything seems lost, some reinforcement that turns the tide. The man who has worked long and intelligently for success often finds it at the very time when the hope of it was forever leaving him ; or, if he does not find it precisely that for which he worked, something better comes to him in its place. Do your duty, hold to your hope, and your darkest hour may be that which announces the dawn of a new day.

SPIRITUAL SELF-RELIANCE

THE men who achieve valuable or permanent results in life are always men of self-reliance,— men, that is, who, instead of accepting the standards and methods of those about them, create standards and methods of their own. These are the men who supply the motive power of society, who give its currents of influence and action direction and force, and who are continually modifying the world in which they work. This kind of self-reliance involves no egotistic elevation of one's judgment above the judgment of his neighbors; it simply involves a clearer insight into the laws of life and a more implicit obedience of them. A man like Marconi finds certain results already achieved through the use of electricity, and certain opinions already formed as to the limitations within which this force can be used. Instead of accepting these results as final, he applies himself to a new study of the force itself, and soon discovers, if not new principles, at least new possibilities of application. He does not reach this result without doubt, hesitation, and long questioning with himself. Upon his own judgment alone he is compelled to make large investments of time, money, ability, and strength. The opinion of those around him is generally adverse to his success; he is regarded as a dreamer, as a man deficient in practical sense and in sound judgment. If he is a sensitive man — and such a man generally is of sensitive temperament — the opinion which surrounds him like an atmosphere imposes a severe struggle upon him, and continually holds a great temptation before him. His weaker self continually implores him to desist and fall into the beaten paths; his strong self, the self upon which he relies, urges him forward. In the end he makes a notable addition to the forces which work for civilization, and he does this through his power of reliance, not upon his weaker but upon his stronger self. The weaker self prompts him to rely upon the judgment of his fellows; the stronger self urges him to rely upon his own personal insight into natural laws, his own personal comprehension of fundamental principles. True self-reliance is dependence upon principles and forces rather than upon current opinion and established judgments. This is the self-reliance which is the possession of all original minds.

There is a spiritual self-reliance which is the secret of great spiritual attainments and achievements. It is the possession of this self-reliance which lifts men in spiritual power above their fellows, which transforms them from mere recipients of influences already in the world into sources of new influences. The man of commonplace spiritual experience and ordinary spiritual strength accepts the standard of those about him, and lives by the laws which govern his fellow-men; the man of spiritual reliance turns away from these things, and trusts his own intuitions of spiritual truth, and his own perception of spiritual realities. His hands, his feet, his heart, his thoughts, are still with his fellow-men; but these are the servants of a new truth and a new power which have come to him, not from looking at his fellows, but at God. If Abraham had been like the men about him, he would have stayed with his flocks and his friends in the fertile lands of his fathers. This was, no doubt, what his lower self prompted him to do; this was his temptation. But he was a man of true spiritual self-reliance. Instead of accepting the standards of his fellows, he trusted his own spiritual intuitions, his own perception of what was right, and his spiritual self-reliance was the beginning of a great history. The same story might be told of Moses, of Isaiah, of Paul, and of every other great religious teacher and reformer. All these leaders trusted to their personal perception of God, of duty, of truth, and not to the perceptions of those who surrounded them. And this is the secret of all religious thinking and living.

THE HIGHEST VALUE ON OURSELVES

DISCOURAGEMENT and despair are the moods in which men make irredeemable mistakes. When hope goes out, the soul is defenceless against its worst enemies. No man commits suicide, either morally or physically, until he believes that he has tried every door of escape, and that they are all barred against him. So long as any light comes into the prison-house in which a man sometimes finds himself, he will grope about for means of escape; it is only when the blackness is absolute that he gives up the fight. No man who believes in God ever has either the occasion or the right to despair; there is for him a calm beyond every storm, however fierce, a sunrise after every night, however dark. It is, nevertheless, very hard, when some great calamity or sorrow is coincident with physical depression, to keep one's heart and to preserve one's faith. There are times when every man must put away the ulterior things for which he has been fighting, and fight simply for life, — that is, for hope. To let in despair is to give up life. We owe it to ourselves to believe always that the best and highest things were intended for us. The man who values himself at a low price will not only receive a corresponding valuation from others, but will finally reduce his actual worth to the price which he has fixed.

Putting the highest possible price on ourselves does not mean that we consider ourselves at the moment worth the price, but it does mean that we intend to make that price represent our actual value to the world. The man who believes that honor and reputation and eminent usefulness are coming to him by and by will not readily give up the future gain for some small bribe which the present offers; will not let sloth and carelessness eat the heart out of his working power; will not be content with small and meagre performance of his duties from day to day; will not limit and hamper his power by some false step, entangling himself finally in the mist which a momentary discouragement has spread about him. It is in times of discouragement and despair, when a man loses sight of his ultimate value, that he commits some lasting mistake, or blights his life with some irredeemable weakness or sin. If in that hour the light of the future could suddenly be shed about him, and he could see himself at the height of his possibilities, the temptation for the moment so attractive and irresistible would seem contemptibly cheap and tawdry, and would be put aside almost without a struggle. That vision, however, comes to us only in our best moments; what we have to do in our weaker moments is to believe in it and live by it, although it is hidden from us. We shall never make any serious mistake or fall into any lasting sin if we can keep this faith burning forever like a lamp in our souls. Put the highest possible value on yourself, and scornfully refuse all those bribes which the present is constantly offering, and the acceptance of which means nothing less than the sale of your future.

PATIENT LOYALTIES

HE must have a very small acquaintance with men and women who doubts the existence of as general and as noble an illustration of heroism to-day as the world has ever seen. There are few families in any civilized community in which there is not some man or woman whose whole life is one of heroic although obscure sacrifice, — the kind of sacrifice which is all the more heroic because it has no other satisfaction than the consciousness of an obligation discharged and a duty performed. There are no more beautiful exhibitions of the finer qualities of human character than are to be found in these patient loyalties ; these devotions of the household, unsustained by any public recognition, uninspired by the hope of any conspicuous achievement, but none the less faithfully persevered in to the end. Stanley's journey through Equatorial Africa oppresses one's imagination with a sense of its indescribable toil and hardship; but the great explorer had the consciousness of doing a piece of work which was not only heroic, but which had world-wide relations and would receive world-wide recognition. There are countless lives which in unbroken continuity of toil parallel Stanley's journey, and yet are unattended by any of the inspiring circumstances which sustained the explorer. For a host of people life means little more than unbroken toil and uninterrupted self-sacrifice, and in many of these cases the beauty of the life lies in the fact that the man or woman who is showing this noble strength is unconscious of any special achievement. It is easy to face great dangers when they last but a little while, and when their successful endurance means recognition and honor; but the patient loyalties of private life, the self-effacement of women for the sake of those in their own household who often have neither comprehension of the sacrifice made for them nor gratitude for it, involve another and a higher kind of courage. In every situation in life there are men and women who are quietly putting their own interests out of sight in order that some other, less vigorous or less fortunate, may be sustained and cared for. These beautiful sacrifices, concealed as they are from the world, constitute a chapter of heroism the like of which has never been written by the splendid daring of war and exploration.

CHERISH YOUR IDEALS

IN every community there are to be found men and women who are steadily moving ahead of the rank and file of their neighbors and companions; every year reveals a wider separation and stamps them with a more aspiring personality. Even the most unobservant begins to feel that there is something unusual about these marked men and women; something which defines them from the mass of commonplace people about them. They are born to rise by the possession of some spiritual quality; some aspiration which by its own impulse lifts them out of their surroundings and sets them in a new world of thought and feeling. It is not necessary that one should be born amid the surroundings of refinement and culture in order to attain the very best results which these things have to give. It is an advantage to be thus born, and to absorb in childhood, by the unconscious process of early education, much that must otherwise be learned ; but this is an advantage which a good many strong natures have missed without apparently suffering any real loss. The making of an intellectual life is always a personal matter. Intelligence, culture, and the resources that come from these attainments lie within the reach of almost every one in this country who gets a clear vision of what he wants and is willing to work for it.

There is something very noble and inspiring in the spectacle, so often presented in American communities, of those who by some finer quality of character or mind are steadily moving away from commonplace life and achieving that personal distinction which belongs to all who live in fellowship with the highest intellectual ideals and in companionship with the finer minds of the world. Such an aspiration is often unrecognized by those who stand nearest and ought to help most; it is often misunderstood and resented as an ambition to be better than one's fellows or one's family; but those who have the real quality can well afford to disregard this lack of sympathy or the criticism which comes from this kind of misinterpretation. A genuine aspiration is never otherwise than noble and unselfish, even when it draws one away from the natural companionships of life,—separates one, that is, not in feeling or in sympathy or in the common fidelities, but in taste and habit and intellectual companionship. No young man or woman need live a commonplace life. There is always an open path to the higher ranges of living for those who are willing to take it. Cherish your aspirations and live by them; they are your real guides; they embody the divine ideal of your life!

THE DENIALS OF GOD

THE suggestion made a few years ago to test the efficacy of prayer by scientific methods excited a great deal of journalistic interest and was widely commented upon, but disclosed from the very beginning lack of insight into the true nature of prayer; for the essence of prayer is not confidence in the ability of the petitioner to bend the Infinite Will or to control the power of the Infinite arm for his own ends. He would be a rash man, essentially unscientific as well as profoundly irreligious, who should venture to set a limit to what is called the direct answer to prayer, — that is to say, the answer in the form in which the prayer is presented; but the essence of prayer is always submission to the Divine Will; it is a petition for what the petitioner believes to be the best good of some person or some cause.

If he could understand that what he asks
for, if granted, would involve great misfortune or serious moral disintegration
to the person or cause, the prayer would
never be made. Now, any intelligent conception of prayer involves this purpose on
the part of the individual, and conceives
of the answer to prayer as being dictated
by the divine insight into the purpose
and needs of the petitioner. For this
reason the silences of God are as significant as those responses which seem so
direct that we can hardly question their
authority; and the denials of God are as
much answers to prayer as are his silences
or his responses. Shakespeare saw this
distinctly, great psychologist as he was,
when he said:

> We, ignorant of ourselves,
> Beg often our own harms, which the wise powers
> Deny us for our good : so find we profit
> By losing of our prayers.

Probably no one will read these words
who cannot look back at some cherished
hope or some passionately loved purpose

the denial of which brought at the moment sorrow and something like despair; that denial, however, seen in the light of to-day, stands out as the greatest piece of good fortune. Many a man has striven for some special position upon which he had set his heart, some special specific opportunity which seemed to him the only open door to fortune, and when the position slipped through his fingers, or the opportunity went in some other direction, it seemed as if life had ended; but, looking back after a decade, it is often evident that the loss of the position and the missing of the opportunity were the very things which opened the way for a higher and broader success. Our prayers are limited by our knowledge, but they are answered out of the wisdom of God. For that reason they are perhaps as often denied as granted, and in the denial the petitioners are most truly heard.

THE SOUL OF WORK

THE first and constant demand of all his employees and co-workers made by a very successful man of business in New York is that their spirit shall be right; so long as their hearts are in the work he cares little for details. Not every man of action is so keen-sighted; most men of this stamp are exacting in matters of discipline, and care little for the spirit in which the work is done. The spirit is, nevertheless, the main thing; if the spirit is right, there will be no shirking, no inefficiency, no procrastination. Where a man's spirit leads him, there will his feet walk willingly and his hands toil gladly. He will need neither urging nor watching; no one will demand so much of him as he will demand of himself; no one will be half so critical of his manner and method as himself. When the motive power is right, the machinery will look after itself; if the motive power is defective or unregulated, the finest machinery is useless. Now, one of the secrets of success is getting one's spirit into one's work; getting behind all one's activities the full force of one's motive power. This is by no means so common as one would think; it is, in fact, so uncommon that when a man puts his whole force into his work he soon attracts attention because by that very fact he separates himself from the crowd.

A great deal of the work of the world is done in a perfunctory manner; done to get through with it; done to secure the return which it promises. It is done without enthusiasm, originality, contagious zeal. Stores, shops, offices, factories, are full of men whose chief desire is to get their work off their hands as quickly and with as little expenditure of

strength as possible. They put as little
of themselves as possible into it. These
are not the men who invent new methods,
perfect new processes, secure rapid and
honorable advancement; they are not
the men upon whom everybody relies,
whom everybody trusts, who turn the
reluctant face of Fortune towards themselves.

The men who give their work character, distinction, perfection, are the men
whose spirit is behind their hands, giving
them a new dexterity. There is no
kind of work, from the merest routine to
the highest creative activity, which does
not receive all that gives it quality from
the spirit in which it is done or fashioned.
Work without spirit is a body without
soul; there is no life in it. Flawless
workmanship is tinsel unless touched by
some influence of the spirit; imperfect
workmanship is often redeemed by the
power of spirit lodged in it. Everything that lacks spirit is mechanical, no
matter how high the grade of its execu-

tion; everything that contains spirit possesses life. To put spirit into one's work is to vitalize it, to give it force, character, originality, distinction. It is to put the stamp of one's nature on it, and the living power of one's soul into it. When Mr. Arnold, in one of his brief speeches in this country, urged young writers to put their hearts into their business, he disclosed one of the sources of his own influence. His technical skill was great, his sense of beauty delicate and almost faultless, his instinct for form unerring; but all these qualities, though they gave his work a great charm, did not give that work its peculiar influence upon many of the finest minds of the day. That influence came from the fact that Mr. Arnold put his spirit into every line he wrote, charged his work with his own personality. It is the quality of spirit which gives his verse its beautiful meditativeness, and his prose its peculiar sincerity and audacity. That which imparts life to the highest artistic work imparts it to every kind of activity to which men set their hands. It is always the man who puts his spirit into his work who makes his work tell for his own success and advancement.

SELF AND OTHERS

THERE is a sublime order in human life as well as in the universe which surrounds and sustains it, — an order which comprehends all needs, co-ordinates all action, and provides for all growth. The chemical relations of matter are but imperfect analogues of the delicacy, the multiplicity, and the inclusiveness of moral relations. All things which men touch through any sense, by any thought, in any act, distil some moral quality and react either for good or ill. We are played upon by influences too many for our comprehension, too delicate for our observation, too far-reaching for our foresight. When we seem to be sacrificing things most precious to us, we are often receiving them back in some finer and imperishable form; when we seem to be working solely for others, we are often serving ourselves in the highest and noblest way.

Doing for others, bearing the burdens of others, identifying ourselves with the struggles and labors of others, help mightily in the working out of our own lives. It is wise to drop resolutely our difficulties at times, to turn aside abruptly from the questions which we are trying to answer; it invigorates the soul and gives the mind a new grip on the perplexing problems. Mathematicians carrying on extended calculations sometimes find themselves forced to clear their minds of figures and betake themselves to some other occupation or amusement; when the mind has recovered its tone, the tangles are swiftly straightened out. Every life needs a large and noble diversion from its perplexities and cares; needs a catholic sympathy with others to preserve it from selfishness, a steady and hearty co-operation with others to give its own work breadth and solidity. No sane man lives for himself; sooner

or later, a life wholly self-centred loses
its soundness and becomes distorted and
diseased. The two elements of self-de-
velopment and care for the interests of
others must be kept in equipoise if harmony, sympathy, and largeness of character are to be secured and maintained.
The true remedy for morbid self-con-
sciousness, the real refuge from personal
grief and loss, are to be found, not in the
monastery, as the old ascetics thought,
but in closer contact with the suffering
world, in more devoted consecration to
the welfare of those about us. There is
no such efficient help for ourselves as
lending a hand to aid our fellows. When
Faust had come to the end of his long
seeking, he found the happiness which
had always eluded him in giving himself
to the service of men. It was not in
self-gratification that the tragic problem
of his life worked itself out, but by large
works for the public welfare. Knowledge, power, and passion failed to satisfy;
it was only when unselfish purpose tri-

umphed over all lower ambitions that peace and victory came. Not to be ministered unto, but to minister, was the aim of the divinest life ever lived among men.

WAIT FOR RESULTS

THE besetting sin of many men is impatience; unwillingness to wait until their experience bears fruit, or their thought has traversed the whole field of fact, before arriving at a final conclusion. This has always been a besetting sin of the race; men have constituted themselves arbiters, and sat in judgment on the universe when their knowledge included only a few facts and covered a very small field. They were ready with the naked eye to formulate the science of astronomy before the telescope had opened up the heavens to them; they hastened to create for themselves images of God before their minds had yet opened to any large revelation of Him; they manufactured systems of theology while they were still ignorant of some of the most important facts concerning them-

selves and the world in which they lived.
Theories of literature and art, once held
and now abandoned, strew the road along
which men have travelled as the deserted
shells line the sea-shore. Only the most
thoughtful and reverent have been content to wait patiently on the Lord ; the
great mass have rushed on and ended in
some dark ignorance which they have
established as a system of knowledge.
It is one of the healthy signs of human
growth that thoughtful men are becoming more and more shy of systems and
theories which claim to be final, and are
holding more and more to what are
known as working theories, — explana-
tions of facts, in other words, which afford
the basis of further observation and reflection. The mere expansion of thought,
without conscious destructive purpose,
has relegated many systems of the past
to the limbo in which are collected all
manner of discarded and worn-out things.
The world and life and literature and art
have disclosed so many new aspects, have

revealed such unsuspected depths, that the most thoughtful men are content to wait for fuller knowledge before attempting a final explanation.

The same impatience is manifested by most of us in our personal experience. We are unwilling to submit ourselves to the discipline of a wisdom larger than our own, to the guidance of a power superior to ourselves. We demand every night an explanation of the events of the day. Every painful experience, every self-denial, every sorrow, wrings from us an impatient cry because we do not understand it at the moment. Our conception of life is so small and mean that we feel as if we ought to be able to understand every part of it from hour to hour. We are not content with the revelation which makes clear to us how to live justly and rightly; we demand that fuller revelation which makes all things plain to thought; we are unwilling to sit as pupils at the feet of Life; we continually demand to be accepted as equals of the great teacher to whose care God has committed us; we refuse to learn the lesson of experience, whose perpetual word is — Be patient. Again and again the years have brought to us the knowledge which the earliest moments of loss and sorrow denied us; but with each new enforced surrender of our purposes and our pleasures we repeat the old blunder; and, instead of waiting patiently until the fruit of the experience has ripened, we interrogate the silence which surrounds us, and when it refuses to answer, we cry out in bitterness and despair. A nobler view of life would make us content and even glad to wait for the larger truths and the deeper joys which an unfolding experience contains for those who are patient and faithful.

AT OUR DOORS

MOST men and women have unselfish impulses; they would
like to serve some good cause or to help
some struggling person. In many cases
these impulses never get beyond the
stage of impulse; they appear on the
horizon of thought and disappear like
beautiful summer clouds; they are radiant, remote, and unfertile. There are
some, however, to whom these unselfish
desires come more frequently, and are
more constantly present, but remain impulse only because there seems to be no
way to make them operative; perpetually
suggesting the performance of a work
which the hand seems unable to do because
the opportunity is apparently lacking.
Such men and women are often envious
of those who have been called to harder
but more unselfish careers. If such work

came to their hand, they are sure they would do it; but what possible service can they perform in their limited field? There never was a greater mistake than that which removes the need and want of the world to a distance; which makes people feel that they are shut out from noble unselfishness of thought and action by reason of the narrow range of activity about them. There is no community so small that there is not room in it for the spirit and work of large-hearted and large-minded men and women; there is no village, no remote neighborhood which does not cry out for the inspiration and help of a great service. The great problems are never at the ends of the earth; they are always at our own doors, and we turn them away as if they were beggars, instead of God's messengers, sent to us with a divine commission for a divine work. First and foremost, it may be the privilege of every man and woman to enrich the community with one of those noble and unselfish natures which are a perpetual ministration of heaven in the world ; those natures which diffuse cheer and light and faith in high things as the sun diffuses heat and power through the whole atmosphere. The value of one noble man or woman in a community is simply incalculable ; no service of the hands, no special work for any cause, is comparable with it in influence and inspiration. The influence of one man who looks over the narrow walls of his own interests and carries the welfare of his neighbors in his heart and mind, is like the falling of the rain which revitalizes every living thing. This noblest service to your kind is open to you. Does your life touch the community in which you live with the power which stimulates every good enterprise ? Does your character mean kindlier feeling, purer religion, better education for and among your neighbors ?

AFTER THE NIGHT

THERE are days in every life when sorrows and troubles that have been fought against and held in control by a strong will overflow all barriers and threaten to overwhelm the soul. Wave after wave of anguish sweeps over one, until every landmark is lost and one prays for death. Such hours have no instant consolation; faith cannot hold them at a distance; activity, courage, consecration, cannot avoid them; they belong to our human life, and they must be endured as part of our human experience. Even Christ was not free from such hours of anguish; the story of the desert, of Gethsemane, of many a lonely mountain-watch, if it could be told or comprehended, would touch the world anew with a sense of gratitude to One who bore our sorrows and carried our griefs. Clearly as the stars of truth and of purpose shone down into the depths of that marvellous nature, there were nights when their light was dimmed by a mist of tears; there were moments, brief but terrible, when the agony was almost too great to be borne.

In the darkness which overshadows us at such times, we are often tempted to cry out, " My God! why hast Thou forsaken me?" The desolation has not only blotted out the joy of the familiar world about us; it has hidden the very heavens, and left us alone and hopeless in the universe. But that cry which seems to have the accent of death in it may be the birth-cry of a nobler life; the God who seemed to have turned away from the cross on Calvary was never so near to humanity as in that awful moment, when the heart-broken sufferer was just about to emerge from darkness into the unbroken light of immortal triumph. His trial, His solitude, His anguish, were all behind Him when that startling cry was wrung from Him; He seemed to be entering Cimmerian night, but He was really on the threshold of eternal day. In our history the same experience is often told; in our Gethsemane blackness seems to have settled down forever, but the splendor of the resurrection morning is only three days removed. Human anguish is real and terrible, as real and terrible for the moment as if it were to be eternal; but, at the longest, how brief it is compared with the sweep and duration of our life! The very memory of those hopeless griefs of childhood which once held us in their grasp has faded; we cannot recall them; or, if we recall them, it is without any sense of pain. Many a bitter disappointment and trial lies behind us, beautiful now as we look back on it, with the light of a purpose higher, and a wisdom wiser than ours. No noble soul ever passes through the night of anguish without finding, as the shadows fall away, a new and heavenly light on the familiar earth. So Savonarola passes into a nobler conception of his mission to men ; so Dante enters into a world untrodden before by human feet; so the nation casts off its burden of wrong, and stands erect, conscious of a new life in its heart and a new and grander work in its hands. The hour on the cross will never be otherwise than unspeakably bitter, but the morning of the resurrection is always just beyond.

SUCCESS IN FAILURE

THE man who has learned to make his failures the omens of success has learned one of the most valuable secrets of life. Some men are discouraged by their failures; they accept the momentary defeat as a final decision against them, and they retire from the struggle disheartened and vanquished. Life has gone against them, and they will strive no more. There are other men, however, to whom failure never suggests anything more disastrous than a wrong method, an imperfect plan, a faulty piece of work. The thought of defeat never comes to them; they will find the defect, remedy it, and strive again. Failure to such men is the discipline which prepares for success, the education which trains for victory. Such momentary defeats lie in the way of every noble conquest in science, literature, art, public life, or practical enterprise. Few great questions are settled at the start, few great reforms are effected in a day, few notable inventions work well on the first trial, few strong men disclose their full power and take their true place by a single brilliant achievement. Slow experimentation, frequent failure, delay, opposition, obstacles, lie along the road to success in every line of work, and remind us constantly that God means that every man shall get character out of his work, even more richly than he gets material reward.

Our thought and our talk about success are rarely spiritual, often purely material. The end of business is to make men; but to hear many business men talk it would seem as if men were made for business only. Anything that interferes with the profits of the year is a calamity, although it may mean the return of moral health to the whole community. There are multitudes who would like to put principles, progress, sentiment,

out of the world because these things are
constantly disturbing the market. They
would rather the curse of slavery should
be perpetuated than that the price of
bonds should be disturbed by agitation ;
they would rather the Irish question
should go unsettled than that the country
should pass through the turmoil of a
general election. Peace at any price is
the cry of these men ; " Keep quiet, and
give us a chance to make money," is
their reply to every appeal for aid in the
struggle against wrong. But God takes
care that the peace which selfishness asks
for shall never come ; movement, change,
progress, are inevitable ; and, so long as
the world stands, these things and the
results that flow from them will baffle
and thwart the schemes and wishes of
those who want the quiet road to a low
and easy success. There is a divine
scorn of our low ideals of success continually manifested in the almost con-
temptuous indifference with which our
carefully elaborated plans are brushed

aside and cast ruthlessly into chaos. God does not stop to explain this constant interference; the rubbish of our mean materialism is not worthy of so much notice. The scheme that would bring us a fortune without work and with considerable loss of honor is whirled out of sight in some sudden tempest of change, and we are left to take the long, arduous road which never brings us to the gold we once craved, but which teaches us to be honest, clean-hearted, humble, patient, and noble. In place of the poor material success that would have made us vulgar and small, we attain a strong and permanent development of character, an understanding of life beside which Golconda is a heap of rubbish, and a nobility of nature beyond price. This is the only real success, and in the winning of it one must look for failures of all kinds.

The chief value of a great and prolonged struggle is oftener in the effort than in the achievement. The great charm of scholarship is in the scholar, and not in his acquirement; the latter serves noble purposes, but its finest result is the man himself. The noblest outcome of a great business career is not the fortune which rewards it, but the probity, sagacity, far-sightedness, and mastery of affairs which it develops in the merchant and financier. A great statesman like Mr. Gladstone renders services to his nation and to civilization of quite incalculable value; but to Mr. Gladstone himself the greatest success he attains lies in the achievement of his character. The other successes he leaves after a little, and as other work presses upon other men the splendor of his performance fades into past history; but the work he has wrought in himself abides as his permanent possession. It can never be taken from him; it is his training and equipment for the eternal hereafter.

There are thousands to whom the immediate success rarely comes; they are met by constant failure and disappointment, they struggle with scant reward and scantier recognition from the world. The sweets of success are never theirs; the struggle, the labor, and the long-deferred hope are their daily experience. Such men need not miss the crowning of life; it may be theirs to pluck from failure the immortal flower of noble character.

GREATER THAN HEREDITY

ONE of the immediate results of modern scientific thought is the deepening sense of the power of heredity and circumstances over individual lives. There is, of course, an immense element of truth in the facts which science has laid bare on this side of human activity, and in the inferences which have been drawn from these facts. No human being is independent of his ancestry, his race, or his age. They supply him with the tools with which he works out his destiny. But it is very easy to over-state this truth; and it is constantly over-stated in current literature. This over-statement, or, perhaps more accurately, this imperfect statement, of the immense force of heredity and surroundings exerts upon many minds a depressing and paralyzing influence. The man who is born with vicious tendencies in his blood, or the man who finds himself on the threshold of his career without the training which other men have received, often feels that defeat is inevitable, and ceases to make any struggle against what he calls destiny. When the teachings of science are interpreted in this way, they become not only pernicious, but absolutely false. Society is full of the refutations of any such conclusion as this. Men have risen to the highest places from origins and influences which seemed specially combined to chain them down forever. The artist must work in the material which he finds at hand, but his conception is his own ; and that, after all, is the soul of his work. He cannot choose his material, but he can always choose the use he will make of it. This is the very citadel of manhood ; when it is once stormed and surrendered, the man may continue to exist, but he ceases to live.

Men to-day need to have their faith in their own power to surmount circum-

stances and to create their careers strength-
ened and deepened. In order that they
may work intelligently, they need to
understand the conditions under which
they are compelled to work ; they need
to know the traits they have inherited,
and they need to discern the kind of
opportunities at hand ; but, above all,
they need a deeper and more vital consciousness that they themselves are greater
than either inheritance or environment ;
and that they were born, not to be made
by these, but to modify and recast them.
Every human life at the bottom is a
revolt against its environment ; every
great reform is a reaction against influences that are at the moment apparently
irresistible ; every great career is a tremendous struggle against existing things ;
and yet great reforms are always on the
way, and great careers are always being
worked out. In every generation there
are born hosts of men and women whose
great service to society is the modification
they make in the existing order of things.

Greater than Heredity

They arrive at usefulness, eminence, and power in the face of circumstances; and they attain these things by virtue of the individual force which lies in every human soul. No man is relieved from responsibility because of that which his ancestors have transmitted to him, or because his own age is inhospitable. No man ought to despair because he is beginning the battle against odds. Every man who makes the honest endeavor to live his own life sooner or later strikes off the chains that bind him, and in making himself free becomes a liberating force in the lives of others.

THE SECRET OF FRESHNESS

ONE of the most serious losses which befall men is the loss of freshness of spirit in dealing with the manifold relationships and duties of life. With the lapse of time there is always danger that the first zest and zeal will pass, and leave us servants of duty or slaves of routine. Joy and enthusiasm fold their wings, and we walk wearily where we once passed with swift and victorious movement. Our business becomes drudgery, our duties onerous, our relations of affection lose the charm of sentiment. There are always a few rare natures who escape the decay which despoils the bloom of life, and carry with them into noon and evening the freshness and splendor of the morning. These are, by virtue of this quality, our guides and inspirers ; they continually renew for us and in us the early vision, the pristine beauty of living. They show us again the loveliness we once saw in the flower, the glory we once saw in the sky, the dignity and nobility which life wore for us before care and selfishness had impaired our finer perceptions.

The joy which such natures preserve for themselves and others, the power of impulse toward high and noble living which they continually generate, do not belong by nature to the few; they are universal gifts, within the reach of all who will put out a hand to take them.

> " 'T is heaven alone that is given away,
> 'T is only God may be had for the asking."

The secret of perpetual freshness in a human soul, of renewing life each day in the beauty of the first creation, lies in the clear and permanent perception of the great spiritual forces and truths of which all visible things are the symbols and revelation. The mother ministers to her child without pause or rest; the long day of her service is divided by no swift-passing hours, and broken by no change of morning into night, or night into morning. Head, heart, hands, and feet are incessantly taxed to care for, develop, and direct the young life. There are times when all these grow weary and would fail if it were not for the consciousness, kept clear and luminous by love, of the inestimable worth of the growing soul that receives all this as its right and does not even think its gratitude. Every true mother understands the spiritual relationship in which she stands to the little group at her feet, and this perception sheds a continual radiance about them and her.

Not less deeply and fruitfully are we all related to our duties, — those incessant demands upon our life which at times almost drain it to the last drop. Met simply from a sense of obligation, without the abiding consciousness of their spiritual significance, they deplete and exhaust us ; but met with the clear insight which discerns the growing purpose of

God behind them, they become transformed and radiant with prophecy and promise; the drudgery of the day is no longer drudgery when one sees in it the slow unfolding of a great new thought for one's life.

In all our relations with the men and women about us there are the same tendency to weariness and the same remedy for it. In the privacy of the home there are, year in and out, the same faces, names, voices, duties, occupation; there is a routine which conceals and at times almost buries the deep and beautiful ties that have made the family imperishable and invulnerable amid the vicissitudes of civilization. They only know the joys which make these relations wells of inspiration and happiness along the journey of life who hold in clear view the rich spiritual relationships of which the family ties are a perpetual and beautiful revelation, a parable repeated from generation to generation with ever-deepening meaning.

Spiritual strength is the only real strength, because it alone is capable of infinite renewal; and in the possession of this strength lies the secret of that freshness of sentiment and zeal which, like dew from heaven, revives the rarest flowers along the path of life and renews day by day the beauty and fragrance of their earliest blooming.

PATIENCE WITH OURSELVES

IT is sound instinct which keeps alive
so well worn a story as that of Bruce
and the spider, — the unconquerable instinct deep in every man and woman to
triumph over obstacles, and to express
personality in positive achievement. The
story of success in the face of constant
and long-repeated failure is a familiar one,
— a story told in lives as illustrious as
those of Lord Nelson and Richard Wag-
ner, and in a thousand lives of which
no public record is made. Patience in
dealing with untoward circumstances and
overcoming objective difficulties is a quality which not only has the honor of all
men, but which brings a certain reward
as the struggle goes on. There is another kind of patience, however, much
more difficult to acquire, and not so
clearly seen and honored, — the patience

demanded of a man by himself. Many
a man who has great power of persistence
in matching himself against outward
obstacles feels constantly depressed and
discouraged when he faces his own nature
and recognizes the return of faults and
tendencies and weaknesses which he
hoped he had overcome and cast out.
No problem is so exacting or demands
for its solution such infinite patience and
persistence as that which is presented to
a man by himself.

If the secrets of all hearts were revealed, it would be found that hosts of
men give up the struggle with themselves
because they have not sufficient patience
with themselves. They become disheartened by their failure to subdue obvious
faults and to cast out evil tendencies.
It is the broken resolution, the deserted
position, the infidelity to a clearly defined
purpose, the unexpected return of the
old temptation in its old force that take
the life and courage out of a great many
men. It seems as if no progress were

being made, as if the battle were an endless round, without issue and without decision. And as there is no struggle so severe and exacting as that which a man has to make with himself, so there is no victory so noble as that which a man wins over himself; for the fact of struggle carries with it the possibility of victory. The spider, reweaving his shattered web for the twentieth time, follows an instinct which those who believe in the presence of God in the world believe to be divine. The man who rebuilds for the hundredth time his shattered purpose and reburnishes his tarnished ideal obeys an instinct from God and may count on God's help, in so far as his struggle is a sincere one. The severity of the struggle and its duration prophesy the permanency of the victory when it is at last won, as a long and exacting process of education implies a very high and unusual degree of proficiency as its reward. Nothing is more difficult than to reform character; but nothing is so permanent as character when it is reformed. The inner struggle which gives life its tremendous meaning and its dramatic interest is not only to the strong, the brilliant, and the versatile; it is more often to those who bear patiently with their own weaknesses, and by patience with themselves secure the eternal victory.

GIVE AND TAKE

PEOPLE of great strength of character are often very difficult to live with. They are to be depended upon in storms, but they are disagreeable in calm weather. No one will underestimate the value of those fundamental qualities of character upon which alone a genuine life or a sound and noble relationship of any sort is built; but there is a great deal more of life than the foundations; there is a whole superstructure of intercourse, relationship, emotions, recreation, and fellowship, and these varied and in a sense lighter things are really not less important than the graver things. Many a man who would go to the stake rather than be guilty of any act of dishonor does not hesitate to crucify those who are nearest him by unrestrained temper; many a woman capable of the highest acts of self-denial feels herself under no obligation to control a tendency to irritability. But irritability may destroy the entire charm of association with the most gifted person, and ungoverned temper has probably involved as much evil to the world in the long run as the direct temptations to sin. A great many men and women live as if there were no such things as differences of temperament; they never take into consideration the moods of those with whom they deal, nor do they ever remember that they have moods of their own; and yet moods have as much to do with making the aspect of life from day to day as the atmosphere has to do with the changing effects of the landscape. There are people to whom the world is one day brilliant with sunshine and the next sombre with shadows, and it is as absurd to ignore this difference as to ignore the changes of weather. The ability to communicate happiness and to aid others lies largely in the power of adaptation, in the keen perception of the temperament and peculiarities of another, and in delicate consideration for temperament and quality. There is nothing more intangible than the sensitiveness of a child, and yet there are very few things more important. The future happiness and success of the child depend largely on the manner in which that sensitiveness is treated by those who stand nearest to it. Many a fine nature is spoiled by the clumsy or brutal hands of those who wreck it as ruthlessly as the hoof of a horse tramples on a rose, and yet whom nothing would tempt to commit any moral wrong against the child. We all demand much for ourselves from others; let us be careful that we honor the demands of others upon ourselves.

WORK THAT NOURISHES

ONE of the secrets of a life of growing power is to be nourished rather than depleted by one's work. Activity is healthful; strain is harmful. Men do not die of overwork, but of maladjustment to the conditions of their work; for under ripe conditions work develops just as truly as exercise, but under wrong conditions it depletes and destroys. The great workers of the world have accumulated force rather than parted with it, and have gathered richness of material and power of action by the putting forth of their energies; so that their lives have moved toward culmination rather than come to an early fruition followed by a long decline. It is easy to detect the difference between the man who is fed by his work and the man who is drained by it. There is an ease, a force, and a zest about the work that nourishes which is never long characteristic of the work that depletes ; for the essential of the work which nourishes is its free and unimpeded expression of the personality of the worker. It is the overflow of his own personal energy, and not the strenuous putting forth of toilsome effort. It is significant that the great artists, as a rule, are immensely productive. Michael Angelo, Raphael, Rubens, Shakespeare, Scott, and men of their class, attest their genius not only by the quality of their work but by its quantity also. This means that they have secured the right adjustment to their conditions, and that work, instead of being a drain, nourishes and develops the worker. The man who works with delight and ease grows by means of his activity, and the first secret to be learned in order to rid work of worry and wear is to take it in a reposeful spirit, to refuse to be hurried, to exchange the sense of being mastered by one's occupation for the consciousness of mastery. To take work easily and quietly, not because one is indifferent to it, but because one is fully equal to it, is to take the first step towards turning work into play.

NOT GETTING BUT GIVING

WITH some exceptions due to special conditions, we ordinarily get what we deserve from our friends and from society; it is idle to charge upon others results due to our own limitations. Men will listen to the man who has something to say worth saying, and will honor and love the man who is worthy of honor and love. If society remains finally indifferent to claims made upon its attention, it is because those claims are not well founded. There is a constant tendency to shift upon others the responsibility which belongs to ourselves, and there are many people who cherish a grievance against their fellows because they are not taken at their own valuation. The public is accused of stupidity because it fails to recognize the political genius which some man finds in himself; editors are charged with prejudice and partiality because they do not open their columns to contributors whose faith in their own gifts is independent of all confirmation from the opinions of others; congregations are declared to be cold and unresponsive because they do not kindle to an eloquence which somehow evaporates between the pulpit and the pew; friends are held to be indifferent because they do not pour out confidences which can never be forced, but which flow freely only when they are drawn out by the subtle sympathy of kinship of nature. It is a false attitude which prompts us to be always demanding, and it defeats itself; we ought, rather, to be always giving. Our friends are powerless to bestow the confidence which does not instinctively flow to us, or to disclose to us those aspects of their lives which are not unconsciously turned to us. Friendship is a very delicate and sensitive relation, and it is absurd to demand from it that which it does not

Not Getting but Giving

freely give. We draw from a friend precisely that which we have the power to understand and enter into; we are shut out from the things which are not naturally our own. If society does not give us what we crave, and our friends do not open to us doors which stand wide to others, instead of indicting others let us look well to ourselves. If we find ourselves losing in strength of position and influence, it will appear, if we search ourselves, that we are not keeping pace with the growth of those around us, and that we are losing ground in the world because we are losing force in ourselves. The whole attitude of those who are continually measuring the returns made to them by society and friends is pernicious; we are here to give, not to get; and they who give largely receive largely.

STRENGTH OUT OF
WEAKNESS

THERE are few things so difficult
to bear as the consciousness of
weakness. It is easy to struggle against
our faults so long as they spring from
some kind of vigor, and we are always
lenient with ourselves in dealing with
those offences which have their root in
energy of nature. These faults do not
discourage us, because we recognize in
them a misdirected force, and we have
faith in our power to give that force new
and wiser direction; but the consciousness of weakness brings a profound sense
of discouragement. It involves the recognition of a real defect in character,
and it carries with it a sense of uncertainty with regard to the future. The
man of strong will has the consciousness
that the strength which has been mis-

guided may itself become a contributing force to the reorganization of his life, but the man of weak will knows that he has to struggle against a fundamental defect. For the weak, however, as for the strong, there is the same law of compensation, — the law under which every possible defect and weakness may be made a source of strength. To be conscious of one's weakness is to put one's self in the way of receiving that which one lacks; for the consciousness of weakness, if acted upon, means steady protection of ourselves against the temptations which overcome us, and in that very act the creation of a new kind of strength. The real measure of character is the amount of moral force produced rather than the moral achievement made. There are men of fundamental weakness who, in the struggle to right themselves, put forth an immense moral force, and by that very fact, although to others they seem to achieve little, they lift themselves out of their weakness into strength. The first step toward strength is the consciousness of weakness. If that consciousness be acted upon, as it may be even by the weakest, then what was weakness begins to give way to a new-born strength, and out of the very quality which promised to destroy the hope of achievement often comes that moral virility which makes the very highest achievements possible. It was the hand which signed the recantation that Cranmer held in the flames that it might be burned first.

WAITING

WAITING for one's chance in life is neither exhilarating nor inspiring, but it is a much more common experience than most men suspect. Nothing is so deceptive to the man who has not yet found his place as the apparently universal success of the men around him; he seems solitary and alone,— an exception to the universal law; he is stranded while all other men are being borne forward by an ample tide of prosperity. But the waiting man has a great deal more companionship than he suspects; almost every one of the men whose careers fill him with a sort of envy has gone through the period through which he is now passing, and which he finds extremely painful and depressing. Very few men make a symmetrical race of life; they do not begin at the start and run steadily to the goal;

there are pauses, interruptions, uncertainties in the case of almost every runner before he really gets into the heat of the contest and begins to take the lead. And these are generally not to be regretted. Many a man looks back upon apparent losses of time and strength in after years and sees that, in his hour of uncertainty and waiting, there were developed in him an endurance, a definiteness of aim, and a patience which have contributed largely, often vitally, to his later success.

Most young men, and especially young men of ample endowments of nature and mind, pass through this period of uncertainty. They are eager to enrol themselves in the great army of workers, but they are not quite sure to which branch of the service they belong. While other men are marching past with flying colors, they are compelled to stand idly by. Many a young man feels at such a moment as if life had deceived him, and he in turn had deceived himself and his friends. The passing hour seems to him an eternal condition; the momentary uncertainty a permanent disability. Such a mood is the only dangerous thing about this trying experience. There is nothing in the fact of being compelled to wait for one's opportunity, nothing in the fact of being undecided at the first as to one's life work, which should fill any man with disappointment. He has only to go to the successful men around him, and secure their confidence, to find that his experience is simply a repetition of theirs. The only danger comes from the beginnings of despair; a despair which sometimes takes the most tragic forms, and sometimes creates a permanent disbelief in one's ability to attain the highest and best things. The young man who was compelled, on the eve of knighthood, to spend a solitary night within chapel walls, used those hours of isolation for the purification of his own soul in order that he might more successfully uphold the right and destroy the wrong. So every young man passing through the painful experience of uncertainty and waiting may find in it a surer knowledge of himself, and a stronger grasp on the certainties of life.

A BEAUTIFUL TALENT

THERE are two maxims of Goethe's which contain the pure gold of truth in one of the most trying relations of life, — our relation to those who are developing gifts and capacities above us: " Against the great superiority of another there is no remedy but love ; " and " To praise a man is to put one's self on his level." In these brief and pithy sayings is contained the whole philosophy of a noble attitude towards superiority of all kinds. There are many who cannot meet the test of having friends and associates pass them in the race by force of greater gifts, and who note the development of talent in others, if not with envy, at least with coldness and silence. In such an attitude there is not only a confession of defeat, but the loss of a great opportunity, — the loss that is always coming to the egotist. A gift of any kind is a resource added to life, a new contribution to the capital which makes society rich. The right-minded man rejoices when the common wealth increases, and finds delight in the work which brings in the added riches; the fact that he lives in a modest house makes him all the more appreciative of the general beauty of the metropolis in which he is a citizen. Moreover, as Goethe suggests, we share in great gifts by recognizing and honoring them. To keep Shakespeare a closed volume because we envy his marvellous power is not to harm Shakespeare but to impoverish ourselves; to take delight in Shakespeare is to partake of his genius and put ourselves on his level. In like manner, to be the first to recognize a dawning superiority in some one who stands near us is not only to give our own nature a beautiful and worthy expression, but to share in the development of a new and inspiring gift. The power of appreciation is itself a beautiful gift, and its culture means the possession of a talent as generous as it is beautiful. To possess it is to drive out the shadow of envy, and to give swift hospitality to truth and beauty. We reveal our own natures by our attitude towards superiority in others.

THE SUPREME SERVICE

ONE of the heresies which mislead us is the belief that we are useful only when we are actually doing something with our hands and feet. The word "doing" is underscored in almost every man's practical philosophy of life; the word "being" is generally written in small characters. No wise man will underrate the importance of activity, because every such man understands that there can be no real life which does not bear fruitage. But the tree does not live consciously for the sake of bearing fruit; the fruit is the overflow of its vitality. We ought to live in the same fashion. Our chief concern ought to be to live deeply, richly, and nobly, and then activity will take care of itself. No one can make the word "being" full of depth and meaning without also giving new depth and meaning to the word "doing." To be great implies the doing of great things, but no man becomes great by an activity outside of himself; he is, first of all, great in himself, and his activity is simply a revelation of his greatness. The first concern of us all is to be noble. The idea that activity is the only measure of usefulness constantly misleads superficial people who are continually doing things with very little thought and very little spiritual force, into the belief that they are attaining great spiritual growth; while, on the other hand, it constantly misleads people who have small strength or small opportunities, and who can do but little with their hands and feet, into the belief that they are of very little use in life. The real measure of greatness is always an inward and spiritual measure. It is a test which cannot be evaded, which dissipates false standards and conventions like the mist, and gets at the very heart of character. The greatest service which any of us can render to our fellows is, first and foremost, to be so evidently strong, earnest, and cheerful that the discouraged take a new lease of hope from us, the doubtful secure a new vision of faith, and those who have fallen a new impulse to get on their feet again. It is of infinitely more importance to-day to pour a new tide of victorious faith and hope and strength into the souls of men than to do anything, anywhere. Beside this supreme service of feeding the spiritual life of the world, all doing, however magnificent, is comparatively insignificant. The greatest servants of humanity are those who, by embodying a noble ideal of life, constantly reinforce the faith of those who are feebler in the possibility of such a life, reconcile them to the hard conditions of their own existence, and inspire them with a faith which of themselves they could not achieve.

LIVE IN TO-DAY

THERE is no illusion so insidious and persistent as that which introduces into the future some element of luck, which stores up for us in the time to come something which we have not secured for ourselves. We are always dreaming of having more time in the future, and of doing things with a strong hand in consequence; to-day we have but fifteen minutes, and what can be made of such a fragment of time? Next year we shall have hours, and then we will read the new books, learn the languages we need to possess, accomplish the larger tasks of which we dream. But the hours never come, and the achievements are made, if they are made at all, in these odds and ends of time that come to us by the way. The wise man is he who knows the value of to-day; he who can estimate to-day rightly may leave the future to take care of itself. For the value of the future depends entirely upon the value attached to to-day; there is no magic in the years to come; nothing can bloom in those fairer fields save that which is sown to-day. The great aim of Christianity is not to teach men the glory of the life to come, but the sacredness of the life that now is; not to make men imagine the beauty of heaven, but to make them realize the divinity of earth; not to unveil the splendor of the Almighty, enthroned among angels, but to reveal deity in the Man of Nazareth. He has mastered the secret of life who has learned the value of the present moment, who sees the beauty of present surroundings, and who recognizes the possibilities of sainthood in his neighbors. To make the most and the best out of to-day is to command the highest resources of the future. For there is no future outside of us; it lies within us, and we make it for ourselves. The heaven of the future, and the hell also,

are in the germ in every human soul;
and no man is appointed to one or the
other, for each appoints himself. To
value to-day, to honor this life, to glorify
humanity is to prepare for eternity, to
seek the eternal life, and to worship God.
The harvest of the future is but the
golden ripening of to-day's sowing.

A HINT FROM A POEM

IN Browning's "Saul," one of the great poems of recent times, there is a fine prophetic motive which gradually develops and becomes clearer until it is seen to be the dominant note of the poem. The simple shepherd, beginning his song with the most familiar things in order to distract the melancholy king, is led on slowly, from strain to strain, the music deepening and widening almost unconsciously until it bursts into the splendid psalm of prophecy; then one becomes suddenly aware that this profounder music was latent in the earliest and simplest notes, and that it is this deep harmony which imparts a thrilling meaning to the whole. The poem is a beautiful parable of every true human life; a parable which becomes more clear and true the more deeply we study it and the more thoroughly we understand our own lives. Every human life begins in association with the most familiar and, apparently, the most trivial things. All its earlier activity is mere play; but from the first hour its little life, like a stream flowing seaward, deepens and broadens; the play becomes educational; the instincts are gradually turned into intelligence; familiar and obvious things become new and strange because seen through fresh experience; finally play becomes work, but work which has still the element of play in it because of the spontaneity and freshness of youth; then come the strain, the responsibilities, the strenuous and unbroken toil of maturity. The mere thoughtless joy of purely physical vitality has gone out of it; pressure and gain, great cares and heavy burdens have come into it. The earlier and melodious notes are no longer heard. But if life has been taken seriously and earnestly, the first melody has given place to an ever-deepening harmony;

living becomes more solemn and awful, not because so much has been lost, but because its possibilities are seen to be so measureless. And now, if one has ears to hear and eyes to see, the prophetic element becomes more and more definite. It is no longer time in which a man is working when this deeper harmony sounds in his heart; it is eternity. As he looks back he sees clearly that from the first careless playtime of childhood this deeper music has always been latent, these profounder notes have formed an undertone which has at last become, not only audible, but dominant. There are times when it would be pleasant to escape the solemnity of life; when we should delight to recall, if we could, the simple joy and pleasure of childhood, with its near hopes, and its immediate aims. But since this is no longer possible, even if it were wise, why not take the profound and sustaining joy which comes with the deeper truth, constantly breaking into the consciousness through

A Hint from a Poem

all our experience, that this hard and at times terrible education is the preparation for something greater than we had ever thought of, the glory of which would blind us if it were to break upon us? We began, like David, with the song of the water bubbling in the brook, and the wind playing on the grass, and the sheep browsing on the hills; let us end, like his song, with the sublime vision of a life redeemed and purified, — a life typified by the Christ.

THE CORRUPTION OF
SELF–PITY

SELF-PITY is the most elusive and deceptive form of selfishness; it beguiles the most acute mind which yields to it, and disintegrates the clearest judgment if it becomes a habit. It is a kind of sentimentalism which finds its food in our vanity and grows by what it feeds on. It seems like a consolation for our mistakes and misfortunes, but it really is an anodyne which protects us from a pain that is essential to health. When we blunder and fail, we ought to suffer, since suffering puts us on the road to a recovery of what we have lost, or to the conquest of that which we have not had the strength to grasp. What we need is the tonic of a relentlessly honest dealing with ourselves. If we have been weak, small, mean, we need to know our defects and call them by names that accurately describe them. If we have not secured the approbation we crave, we ought, for character's sake, frankly and fully to accept the fact that we have missed the approbation because we have not done the work that would have won it. If we deal with ourselves in this spirit, we pay ourselves the highest respect and put ourselves in the way of being worthy of it.

Too many of us do nothing of the kind. We begin to pity ourselves, to look upon others as ungenerous and unsympathetic, to lay the responsibility for our failures on some person or circumstance. We soon come to think of ourselves as martyrs and victims; we build up a fictitious character for ourselves; we create unreal sorrows and bear unreal wrongs. We end by corrupting and debilitating ourselves to such a degree that we cease to have a clear vision, a truthful tongue, or a loyal heart. To put the result of a course of self-pity in plain speech: we deceive ourselves so long and so persistently that we become chronic liars to ourselves and chronic slanderers of others; and it is an awful thing to become an incarnate lie in a universe which is relentlessly truthful.

THE REAL POWER IN LIFE

THERE is no mechanism so delicate as the adjustment of forces which make up a human life. The most exquisite mechanical adaptations represent but grossly the fineness of moral, intellectual, and physical adjustments which are ultimately secured in every human life. If we could only realize for one hour how subtle, manifold, and exacting are the influences which shape us, there would be far less trifling with the serious concerns of character. If we could really feel that every sin, every negligence, every neglect, involves either a permanent or a passing loss of power, and that we are absolutely powerless to sever ourselves from the causes which we set in motion, we should walk with very careful feet. That which gives us the power of impressing our fellows is not so much the conscious direction of our abilities as the unconscious expression of ourselves. It is character in its continuous revelation which gives or denies us the power we seek with others. There is no possibility of concealing one's real self; it will discover itself, and in that discovery, constantly going on, lies our chief influence, either for good or ill. The only way to make the most of ourselves is to hold ourselves in perfect humility to loyalty and obedience. There is a greater power behind us, ready to be expressed through us, than we can comprehend. Men who take their lives into their own hands, who obey or disobey as they choose, and use their gifts as forces which they can, in a way, detach from themselves, are continually coming to failure, if not to positive disaster. It was once said of a public man of great intellectual force, but exceedingly questionable moral character, who was put upon his defence by certain charges, that when he stood on his feet and spoke for himself it seemed as if no evidence could convict him, but when he sat down and was silent, it seemed as if he had no friends and no defence. This man had detached his gifts from his character. When he could employ them consciously he made an impression, but the moment he was silent, his power was gone. There was no unconscious atmosphere of truth and integrity about him. His character belied his gifts. We ought so to live that the great purpose behind us may work itself out through us, and that, whether speaking or silent, whether working or at rest, the unconscious atmosphere which we carry with us may breathe purity, fidelity, and loyalty.

THE GRACE OF OPPOR-
TUNITY

THERE are no men or women who owe more to themselves and their fellows than those to whom opportunities are constantly coming, before whom doors are constantly opened. Such a lot is the highest of all good fortunes, since it means not only success, but growth; not only talent, but the possibilities of character. There is a patient host who work on, day after day, with no hope of large advancement, no stimulus of marked progress, and no inspiration of wider outlook; who must find their reward in the consciousness of work well done, and possess their hearts in patience, as far as their aspirations and ambitions are concerned. Many a man is conscious of a larger power than circumstances afford him the room to put forth; and it involves no small strain on character to accept such limitations cheerfully, and to recognize the progress of those who are more fortunately placed, not only without envy, but with a generous pleasure. He who can do this has a heroic strain in him.

To those, therefore, into whose hands the golden keys are put, there come not only great satisfactions but great responsibilities. If such an one is tempted to find the secret of his success in himself, let him consider well what his circumstances have been, and let him think always of the nobler men who are bound in creeks and shallows while he spreads his sail on the open sea. Every new opportunity should send a man to his knees instead of lifting him up in his own mind, should give him additional poise and balance instead of access of vanity. Nothing is more painful than the spectacle of one whom a little success makes self-conscious and inflated, so that the larger the success which comes the plainer becomes his essential weakness.

On the other hand, there is nothing which comforts those who are striving with adverse conditions so entirely as the untainted and unspoiled spirit which receives success as a trust, not as a reward, and bears it as a possession to be divided rather than hoarded.

FORGETTING THE THINGS
THAT ARE BEHIND

AN army which is to move rapidly and strike swift, decisive blows carries as little baggage as possible. It leaves all impedimenta in the rear, and relies for its safety upon its ability to move with sufficient rapidity and force to overcome obstacles. An old-time Oriental army carried with it every sort of convenience and luxury; a modern Occidental army discards everything but the weapons and the supplies which equip it for action. There are a great many people who move encumbered with as much impedimenta as the Persian armies which the Greeks once destroyed. They leave nothing behind them; their mistakes, blunders, and failures are carried along from day to day as if they were priceless possessions instead of being shells which ought to have been thrown by the wayside long ago, after the fruit of experience has been taken from them. There is a grace in forgetting as well as in remembering; there is a genius in knowing what to discard as well as what to keep; and both these are the invariable possession of a successful and efficient life. No man of conscience can forget his sins; no man of judgment can forget his mistakes; but he does not carry them with him. What he does carry is the experience which has come to him through them, — the strength, the wisdom, the grace of character, which have been developed by what they have brought or what they have taken away.

A man's real life is always before him; the past is only valuable for what we can learn from it. The days fade from all distinct recollection because these artificial divisions of time are of no consequence except as character has grown or degenerated in them. A man's greatest achievement, once accomplished, begins immediately to recede and become less and less in his eyes. No really great man has ever reposed on anything which he has done ; there has always been the consciousness that he was greater than any expression he had given of himself, and that the real satisfaction and joy of his life lay, not in the work, but in the doing of it. One task succeeds another, one experience follows another, in endless succession ; a man's work is never finally done, because his life is always expanding ; and the time will never come when this law of progression will cease to operate. There can be no heaven which is not a heaven of development. It is a great waste of strength to make one's faults and blunders and sin impedimenta in the onward march. There is no virtue in continually bemoaning the misdoings of the past. Real repentance is not lamentation, but girding up the loins for the work of expiation. Let the dead old year bury its dead ; leave behind the depressing memories of failure and defeat, while you carry their lessons in your heart. Your real life is not behind, but before you; it is the new year and not the old which is your opportunity.

BELIEVE IN YOUR WORK

THE English governor of one of
the provinces of the British Em-
pire in India, commenting on his good
fortune in getting out of the country
before the breaking out of the Mutiny,
said : "I could never have fought well,
for I could never make up my mind
whether our conquest of India was a
divinely inspired act or a great dacoity."
The remark showed sound knowledge
of life. No man can fight vigorously
and successfully if he is uncertain of his
right to fight. The soldier who leaves
behind him the open question whether
a thing ought to be done or not, in nine
cases out of ten will retreat along that
line. The advance line is held only by
the man who believes in the end that lies
before him, and in his right to secure
that end. Nothing blights faith in a
purpose, or saps the strength to carry

it out like skepticism. The skepticism need not be very deep or very radical; a very little of it will go a long way in destroying a man's working power. It is one of the mental and spiritual misfortunes of our time that so many men and women are uncertain whether the thing they are doing is worth while. They are fighting a losing battle, not because they have not the force or the equipment to fight a winning one, but because they can never quite make up their minds whether the fight ought to be made or not. A half-hearted or questioning Stanley would be an absurdity. The man who is to cross Africa through the heart of its vast forests and its deadly morasses must be a man who believes that doing that particular thing is worth every exertion that a human being can make, and that if his life goes into the work the loss will be well made. No smaller faith than this could have given Stanley the impulse which sent him through the heart of Africa. If Mr. Edison spent his nights in querying whether his work by day was worth the doing, the wonderful development of the practical use of electricity which he has secured for the benefit of men would never have been made. Doubt is a healthy stage in the life of every man who thinks, but it is only a stage, not a permanent condition. Sooner or later the man who achieves anything in life leaves doubt behind him and puts his hand in the resolute grasp of a clean, clear, triumphant faith in some cause or purpose, or principle or aim. When we stop to ask ourselves whether life is worth living, we ought at once to call in the family physician; that question means disease either of body or mind; it is a question which no healthy man or woman has any business to ask.

EARN YOUR SUCCESS

ONE of the most futile things in life is the attempt to make men fill places for which they are not fitted, or to do work to which they are not equal. There are few things which cause so much disappointment and general irritation as the mistaken acts of friendship which push a man higher than he can stand, and, in a blind desire to serve him, load him down with responsibilities which he cannot bear. A true friendship is always wise and candid. It recognizes the limitations of one whom it would aid, and does not endeavor to pass over those limitations and set at naught that general law of life which establishes an affinity between a man's capacity and the work he is to do. There is, in fact, very little that friendship can do for a man beyond securing him a good opportunity; it cannot, with the best intentions and the utmost zeal, make him equal to the opportunity. Friendship stands at the door and holds it open, but it cannot make him who enters at home in a new place unless there is that within himself which makes it possible for him to adapt himself to his new surroundings. There are a great many men who seem to think that, by the assistance of their friends, all things are possible to them, and who hold their friends responsible for their failure to secure the places and emoluments which they believe are their due. Such persons are entirely ignorant of that great law of life which imposes upon each man the necessity of working out his own salvation. Character can never be formed by deputy, nor can great works be done, great responsibilities met, and great results realized, by delegation to another. For our opportunities we may well look to our friends; for our successful dealing with our opportunities we must look to ourselves.

Friendship can put a man in the right place and give him the proper tools, but it cannot direct his work, nor can it bring out the skill which Nature has denied or which inefficiency has refused to acquire.

There is a broad justice running through life which is only the more apparent because one sometimes finds exceptions to it. As a rule, men achieve the success which they deserve, and obtain the places for which they are fitted. There are some who, by the accidents of the time in which they live, are thwarted of results which might properly have been theirs under more favorable conditions; but the great majority of those who fail are responsible for their failures. Their intentions may have been good, but they have lacked either the wise discernment of their duties or the resolute industry which turns opportunity into achievement. A Napoleon without social or political backing will somehow come to the head of the army and will use it as if it were a part of himself; a

Earn Your Success

McClellan, with the best intentions in the world and the most sincere patriotism, when every possible instrument of success is put into his hand, will remain paralyzed and, to a large degree, impotent. He had the opportunity, but it was too great for him; and, in the light of history it is seen to be a misfortune that he was advanced to a place which he could not hold, and from which he could not progress. All that we can ask justly from our most devoted friends is that they shall help us to the possession of the things we need to work with. When they have done that, we can ask nothing more of them which they can wisely render to us. If we fail, the responsibility is upon us and not upon them. Neither their love, their services, nor their resources can fit us for positions to which Nature, or our own inefficiency has not made us equal. It is easy to lay to our souls the flattery of having been defeated by forces against which no human will could have striven successfully, or to have been thwarted in our effort to work out whatever is in us by lack of opportunities; but if we analyze the causes of our failure honestly, we shall generally find that they have been due to some defect in ourselves — a defect which could not have been remedied by all the friendship and co-operation in the world, and a defect which ought not to have been remedied by any one but ourselves. There is a fundamental immorality in the attainment of success for which a man has not striven; there is an element of falsehood in the holding of a place which has not come to one as a recognition of his ability to fill it. Better a thousand times obscurity and humble work than prominence or opulence gained by accident or secured by favor. There is a kind of aid which it is immoral for a friend to give and equally immoral for another to receive; it is the aid which takes the place of some work we ought to have done, some energy we ought to have put forth, some strength and power

of character we ought to have attained.
No success is real or lasting, or worth
having which does not come as the outward recognition of some inward quality
in the man who achieves it.

LIGHT IN THE SHADOW

THERE is nothing comparable in interest with the development of a human life. The love of biography, so widely diffused, bears constant testimony to the recognition by men at large of the supreme importance of the unfolding of personal character. The story of the man who begins with small opportunities in boyhood, and, by patience, integrity, courage, and submission, comes at last to great place, noble character, and large usefulness, is the one story in which men never lose their interest, and which constantly recreates hope and ambition in struggling and despondent souls. Such a story not only teaches the lesson of the power of steadfast purpose and continuous energy, but always bears witness to the presence of something behind the man, greater than he, wiser, more far-seeing; something which takes into account the largest possibilities of his nature and which, by hope, by impulse, and by pressure, pushes him constantly onward. In every great career two elements are combined — the element of powerful personality, and the element of strength, of plan, and of energy outside and above the man.

Looking at a successful career from the outside, it seems as if the course of such a career were perfectly plain; as if the man saw from the beginning what he could attain to, and so, because he saw the remote end, was able to surmount cheerfully all obstacles, to pass through all difficulties, and to maintain an unshaken courage in all adversities. But this is really never the case. There are times in the lives of the greatest men when aims become indistinct, when hopes wither and courage faints; times when the man works, not because he sees whither he is going, or what he shall accomplish, but simply in blind reliance or in desperate resolution. It is these dark experiences, common to all men, great and small, which seem to serve as avenues of access to heart and mind for the deepest teaching of life. When a man's career is taken out of his own hands, when the consciousness of weakness is borne on him so strongly that he feels as if the very foundations had failed, there often comes with this absolute giving up of all resource in one's self the vision of a greater power, the glimpse of a diviner purpose in which the individual life is folded and toward the realization of which it is borne irresistibly forward. The supreme comfort of life lies in this clear perception of the tremendous educative power and purpose behind it — an influence which no man can escape, and which he can defeat only by his own infidelity. It is a great thing to feel, when our own small plans are in a moment destroyed, our own ambitions in a moment thwarted forever, that, instead of losing, we are exchanging a lower for a higher thing;

that the fall of the blossom means the coming of the fruit. An educative process is always a painful one, involving constant self-denial, self-surrender, self-abnegation; but there is nothing in life that so dignifies and ennobles a man; nothing which in the end crowns him with such enduring success. One can well afford to stand at times, baffled and heartsick, to feel that nothing is certain, that one's plans and hopes may in an instant be blotted out, if with this sense of weakness there also comes the sense that a higher power is directing one's career, and that through these painful experiences the unseen God is transforming a lower into a higher conception of life, opening up a soul to new and greater truth, and lifting one through shadow into his own light.

THE WASTE OF FRICTION

UNDOUBTEDLY a great many people overwork, but there are a great many sins laid on the shoulders of work which ought to be bound on the back of friction. Friction kills ten men where overwork kills one; friction destroys freshness, wastes energy, spends courage, and induces failure. Except in cases where personal adjustments are absolutely necessary, friction is pure waste, serves no purpose, accomplishes no result, and is so much capital of health, strength, high spirit, and good working power thrown away. It is safe to say that no great enterprise ever succeeded in which friction was not reduced to a minimum, because friction involves necessarily defective organization or antagonistic methods and plans. The home in which friction is a permanent element is a caricature of a real home.

The Waste of Friction

It is a home without repose, without cheerfulness, without that atmosphere of confidence, sweetness, and sacrifice which is to all the best and noblest interests of the family what the air is to plants and men. Incidental and occasional friction are inevitable ; continuous friction means bad organization, unsympathetic workers, or the presence of obstinacy, stupidity, or wilfulness. Wherever it exists it ought to be taken as an indication that there is something wrong, and as a suggestion that it is time to examine the situation and remove the obstacle. In most cases the observance of a few simple principles will eliminate this exasperating source of weakness and failure.

It is useless for people to try to accomplish a common result without mutual confidence in one another. If a man lacks confidence in his partners he would better dissolve the partnership and form new business connections ; if a man lacks confidence in his friends, he would better examine himself to see whether he is worthy of association with them, and if he can satisfy his mind on that point he would better cease intercourse with them rather than carry it on at the expense of that good understanding which is the basis of all true friendship. A friendship accompanied by incessant irritation will sooner or later come to an end, and the sooner that end is reached the better. Mutual confidence is the only sound and healthy basis for co-operation in any enterprise. When we cease to have confidence in one another, it is time that the connection should be broken.

Thorough-going sympathy makes friction impossible, and is at the same time the foundation rock on which all great success is builded. No man can co-operate, heart and soul, with another unless he has sympathy with his aims and spirit. He cannot even understand what those aims and spirit are without the power to put himself in the other's place and see things from his point of view. Great enterprises go through to success when men come into full sympathy with one another in their devotion to a great purpose. Such a sympathy is a silent but infallible interpreter between men who may differ in many points, urge diverse methods, even possess antagonistic temperaments, and yet be perfectly harmonious through their agreement in some central purpose.

Every great work is, in a certain sense, a compromise. No man is able to achieve a great thing with his own unaided hand. At some point or another he needs the help of others, and when he needs that help he must concede something to secure it. It is only under a despotism, or under some form of slavery that one man arbitrarily imposes his will on another. In that case there is no friction, because there is no individuality, no consciousness of manhood, no barrier of self-respect. Mutual concessions are the price which men must pay for co-operation, and in the end they gain more than they lose; for many a man who has genius for ideas is helpless without the practical skill which can give them shape and form. In the shaping and forming, the idea is generally modified to advantage.

Men who work together and without friction must respect one another. There is nothing which creates so effective an *esprit de corps*, which develops so thorough a discipline, as the common respect of each man for the place, responsibilities, and authority of every other man.

DISCIPLINE OF HINDRANCE

THERE is an instinctive feeling in the heart of every man that he has a right to a clear opportunity to do his work in the world and bring out in full measure whatever force there is in him. It is this instinct which resents the obstruction of obstacles as something foreign to life, as accidents which break up the general order of things, as useless interferences which weaken effort, delay achievement, and exhaust strength. Every man craves a free field for his work, and a clear opportunity for his talent. If these are granted he is confident of the success which would crown his efforts; if these are secured he is certain of the useful and victorious life which he will lead. Every energy and gift contains within it an impulse for action. The man who discovers in himself the ability to write feels that the opportunity to write ought to be given to him; the man who develops a gift for oratory craves the opportunity of the platform, and feels wronged if he does not secure it; the man who is conscious of great executive force demands an ample field in which to exercise it, and feels defrauded if he does not secure it. Behind every gift there is usually an energy sufficient to send it with the impulsion which powder gives to the ball.

If success in life lay entirely in the working out of one's gifts symmetrically, and in doing one's work with the completeness and finish of a fine piece of mechanism, obstacles and limitations would be interferences with the normal order of things, obstructions thrown in the way of the runner which ought not to be there. But real success is not a matter of complete and symmetrical achievement; it is the outcome of a man's life when the normal force within him is measured against the difficulties he has to overcome. These obstacles, which seem so unnecessary, these constantly recurring, vexatious, and often meaningless interruptions, serve a high moral purpose in our lives. There is no business, profession, or art which is not beset by them. In one of his most interesting and suggestive chapters Mr. Hamerton emphasizes the moral qualities which the technical difficulties in painting bring out in an artist. Instead of being able, without flaw, interruption, or break in the effort to put on canvas the perfect representation of the ideal picture in his own soul, the artist is obliged to overcome all manner of small, vexatious difficulties in the mere mechanical work of putting his vision into a visible form. But in surmounting these difficulties, vexatious as they are, the vision becomes clearer, the purpose stronger, the will steadier; and when the work is done, there is a moral as well as an artistic quality in it. Interruptions and obstacles arising from the details which abound in

every occupation, which grow out of difficulties of personal adjustment, out of
variations of physical condition, out of
changing moods and diverse temperaments, are vexatious and exhausting, but
they play a great part in our lives, and
the spirit in which we meet them largely
determines our character. Many a man
puts forth more moral strength in remov-
ing obstacles from his path than another
puts forth in achieving the highest distinction. In such a case, who shall say
that the man whose whole effort has been
spent in clearing his way has not done as
much and won as noble a success as he
who has run with swift and unencum-
bered feet to the goal at the end?

THE LIMITS OF HELP-
FULNESS

FRIENDSHIP is not only one of
the greatest delights and resources
in life, but it offers some of the finest
opportunities which fall to the lot of
man. No man can feel poor or entirely
bereft so long as he has faithful friends ;
no man can feel that he has made a
failure of life so long as he is able to
attach strong, high-minded men and
women to himself. But friendship, like
all the other good gifts of life, ought to
be accepted rather for what one can put
into it than for what one can get out of
it. There are times when we must lean
heavily on our friends, — when we can
do nothing for them and they can do
much for us. But the normal attitude
of every man toward his friends ought
to be that of giving rather than of get-

ting, of serving rather than of being served. It is of the first importance that the service we render our friends shall be intelligent, — not simply a blind attempt to help in ways which are essentially unhelpful. It is often said that nothing requires so much wisdom as the bestowal of money; it might be added that few things require greater tact and judgment than the rendering of the services of friendship.

A really noble friendship, which realizes the higher ideals of the relation, must be open-eyed; friendship ought never to lose its sight. Our friendship is really helpful to others, not when it makes things easy for them, gratifying their desires and yielding to their humors, but when it develops the best that is in them; when it puts them on their mettle, makes their weaknesses clear, and spurs them to the acquirement of the strength which overcomes. "Our friends," said Emerson, with characteristic insight, "are those who make us do what we can."

The Limits of Helpfulness

Our real friend is not the man or woman who smoothes over our difficulties, throws a cloak over our failings, stands between us and the penalties which our mistakes have brought upon us; but the man or woman who makes us understand ourselves and helps us to better things. It is a great mistake to be fettered by the weaknesses of our friends, to accept their limitations as our own, and, by yielding to their moods and narrowness, to circumscribe our own life. No healthy nature is willing to allow another to take toward it the relation of a parasite; a healthy nature demands health in others; it is willing to bear any number of burdens for others, to put its strength in the place of another's weakness; but it is never willing that another should come so to rely upon it that the life of that other is dwarfed and enfeebled. A self-respecting friendship demands that there shall be equality between the two who are bound by it; that each shall give as well as receive, and that each shall furnish a part of the capital of the mutual investment. If our friends press too closely upon our individuality, our privacy, or our work, it is the part of friendship to repel the intrusion. There are certain limits beyond which even friendship cannot go; when it does, it has become morbid and unhealthy, and is debilitating alike to him who leans and to him who supports.

That which a true friendship longs for and strives to achieve is the growth of power and freedom in another. It will not hesitate to give pain because it must be based on truth. Drawn upon sometimes for self-pity, it will not shrink from the sting which arouses energy and dignity; it will have too much respect for another to permit in that other any decline from the dignity of a true personality, from the independence which belongs to real character. It will not permit itself to be made the tool of another's weakness, the slave of another's humor; it will resolutely hold its own.

The Limits of Helpfulness

The truest hospitality sometimes consists in locking the door, and the truest friendship sometimes involves absolute unresponsiveness to an appeal that ought never to have been made. If you wish to serve your friend, help him to be self-supporting, but do not let him become dependent upon you. Sting him, if necessary, into the consciousness of his own weaknesses, even if it cost his goodwill. The surrender of a friendship for such a reason may sometimes be the highest evidence of its purity and nobility.

HEALTHY DISCONTENT

THERE is a discontent which para-
lyzes and destroys; a discontent
with one's conditions and circumstances
which makes one restless, bitter, and in-
efficient. This is always a moral disease
to be avoided, as any other contagion is
avoided, and to be cured as any other
disease is cured. But there is another
kind of discontent which is a spur to
excellence and an inspiration to achievement.— discontent with one's self. No
man ought to be contented with himself,
to be satisfied with the work he has done
and the place he has secured. It is the
prevalence of self-content in these matters
that gives us so many average men and
women, so many commonplace persons
who mistake their prejudices for convictions and their ignorance for knowledge ;
men and women who desire no other

authority for a statement than that they
believe it, and who see no truth in the
world which does not belong to them.
This kind of self-sufficiency breeds egotism, narrowness, and ends in absolute
arrest of development. No man can
grow who is satisfied with himself. The
open-minded man is never free from the
feeling that he has not done as much as
he ought, and that his future must redeem
by its increased usefulness and activity a
past in which he has failed to do the best
and the most for himself and for others.
It would be found, if one could look
into the hearts of the men and women
whose course through life is a steady
progression upward, that a divine discontent is forever present in aspiring
spirits. Those who rise are never satisfied with themselves, but are always finding defects, faults, and failures to humble
them and to make them more strenuous
in that which lies before them. It is a
great mistake to be always telling persons and nations that they have attained

great things, and that they have made some approach to perfection. The kind of criticism Mr. Arnold gave us is a great deal truer and more helpful than the adulation and undiscriminating commendation which some other travellers have given us. Recognition of work done is a spur and a help; but there ought always to go with commendation, both to persons and to peoples, a clear setting forth of the better things still to be done. "The love of doing and the scorn of done" is the only safe feeling.

LOVE AND WORK

L OVE and work are often far apart in our thoughts, but it is only when they are united that the highest results are achieved. Duty and necessity will make men faithful, but never inspire them. Love, on the other hand, adds to absolute fidelity a glow and inspiration which are creative. Those who have studied Corot's skies, deep and tender with an unfathomable light, have often wondered why this artist alone of all his contemporaries has mastered the secret of the morning sky. But they have ceased to wonder when they read of the passion for the sky of the dawn which possessed the great painter, and led him, morning after morning, year after year, into the open fields, to sit there, absorbed and enchanted, while the night slowly changed to day about him. Corot loved the dawn, and the dawn inspired him as it has inspired no other artist. It is the absence of love which makes most work drudgery. A good deal of that which is put by necessity into men's hands to do cannot of itself evoke this feeling; there is nothing in it which touches the imagination or appeals to the emotions. When the work itself does not possess these qualities, it can still be done in the spirit which inspires them. A man may love life and all that it brings him in the way of opportunity with such intensity and whole-heartedness that the meanest detail of it comes to have meaning and beauty in his eyes. All great workers who have achieved the very highest results and have stamped their performances with individuality and distinction, have been men of a mighty passion; they have been enchanted by the thing they were doing; and their devotion to it, their absorption in it, have betrayed the marks of a great affection.

There is a great deal of work, how-

ever, given to men to do which is capable
of calling out the deepest sentiment of
love, which has in it suggestions for the
intellect, appeals to the imagination, out-
looks for usefulness, sufficient to lay a
spell on the greatest nature that ever
handled tools. So, no one can doubt
who looks at his canvases, did the work
of painting appeal to Raphael; so, un-
questionably, did the work of writing
throw its spell over the great soul who
passed through three worlds in order that
he might see man in all the conditions
of his estate. The same mighty passion
is found in the achievement of every
great worker, and every great man must
of necessity be a great worker. No
mere sense of duty, no whip of necessity,
could ever have drawn out such a magnificent and unbroken activity as that which
made the history of Mr. Gladstone.
We all need to come into closer contact
with our work. It is not enough to
make a sense of duty wait upon it; it is
not enough to brood over it in thought,

penetrating it with ideas, and giving it the order of a new and fresher method; we must press it to our hearts if, for ourselves and for others, we would transform what might be its drudgery into the discipline that makes character, and transmute its hard materialism into something spiritual and satisfying.

ASPIRATION AND AMBITION

ASPIRATION and ambition represent two very different motives and attitudes, although they are often confused in popular speech. The ambitious man, by reason of the purely selfish character of the underlying principle of his life, may be entirely devoid of aspiration, although the brilliancy of his career often confuses the minds of people and conveys the impression that he possesses that which is in no sense his. The aspiring man, on the other hand, is often accused of ambition, although of this last infirmity of great minds he may lack even the average endowment. In fact, nothing creates more confusion in life than this inability to discern between the fundamental motives of different lives. Acts which are identical in appearance are often so widely separated in motive that they are entirely blameworthy in one instance and entirely praiseworthy in the other. The ambitious man desires advancement, and place and wealth and influence, because these things contribute to some purpose apart from the growth of his own character; because these are so many keys with which he proposes to unlock the treasure-house of life, although when these treasures lie within his hand he has no thought about their use except a selfish one. The aspiring man, on the other hand, cares most of all for the development of his own nature; his desire is not to get the most out of life, like Falstaff, but to put the most into it, like Paul or Luther. He feels the steady pressure of the highest impulses upon his soul; he recognizes the constant solicitation of the noblest opportunities, and he responds to the one and pours himself into the other, not for what they shall give him, but for what, through them, he shall bestow upon the others.

The true artist is not the man who

waits eagerly for recognition, or who
studies the popular taste to find out by
what trick of his brush he may make
sure of frequent appearance on the line
at the exhibition ; the true artist is con-
sumed by a mighty thirst for beauty,
impelled by a mighty impulse to express
that which lies within the vision of his
own soul. The true man of letters is
not he who studies the fluctuations of
taste and furnishes wares for the market,
but he who feels the irresistible impulse
of some great truth seeking for expression through him ; such an one is
constantly under the spell of the master-
teacher, Life, and, as a sincere and single-
hearted pupil, has no other desire but to
learn and speak the truth. An aspiring
man stands in small need of the praise
of his contemporaries or the regard of
the multitude ; although these are not
without satisfaction and use to him, his
main purpose is with himself in the
noblest sense. He feels that he has
been intrusted with a great and rare gift,

and that his life work is not to seek that
which shall gratify his pride or his vanity,
but to bring out symmetrically, beauti-
fully, and purely that which lies like an
unspent and undeveloped power within
himself.   An aspiring life, wisely lived,
in the end brings its own external rewards and recognition ; and the man of
aspiration can wear safely all the honors
which the world chooses to put upon
him.   These things come to him, not as
objects external to himself, which he has
grasped with selfish hands, but as the
normal fruit of the ripening of his own
life ; there is no poison in them for him ;
there is no power of seduction in them ;
they cannot satisfy, nor can they arrest
his career.   When he has secured them
all they are as nothing to him, because
his life is still to go on in higher ventures
and to more remote ends.

What is needed in the world is not
ambition but aspiration ; not men who
are seeking office and power and wealth
for themselves, but men whose overflow

of energy and intelligence and whose creative work and influence produce these things as naturally as the orchard produces its autumnal fruit. In the long run the world knows its great men, and knows that they are men of aspiration. It is true that aspiration is sometimes mixed with ambition; but it is also true that the work of a man's hand or brain which remains a permanent possession to humanity is always the expression of the truth that was in him, and not of the falsehood; sooner or later that which was false passes away, and only that which was true remains. In business, in the professions, in art, in literature, and in public life, it is the aspiring man who is the natural and only safe leader; he is the man who is ready to say with Lincoln: "If this sentence in my message is true I would rather fail with it then succeed by suppression of it." He is ready, with Gladstone, to go out of office for a principle, but he is never ready to remain in office without one.

Works and Days

Aspiration is the one quality which makes life cumulative, which forbids any halting in the long career of growth, which, without resting and without hasting, impels a man onward to the complete unfolding of himself. The aspiring man never rests content with any performance, however the world may applaud. To him all the works of his hands are inadequate — there is always something more in his mind than he has been able to express; there is always something nobler in his conception than his hand has conveyed to the eyes of others. When fame comes to him it does not build a wall of caution about him and lock its gates upon his courage and his independence; it spurs him on to still nobler efforts; instead of being an anchor which holds him stationary in some fair and peaceful port, it is a sail which bears him still seaward with the illimitable ocean before him.

THE GRACE OF ACCEPTANCE

THERE are many sincere and honorable men and women, with a fine sense of independence, who are generous in giving and niggardly in receiving; who bestow upon others with a liberal hand, but who find it hard to accept those services and kindnesses which they love to bestow. But one cannot be really generous who refuses to his fellows the pleasure he takes to himself. There is nothing within one's reach quite so satisfying as throwing a door of opportunity open to some one who stands in sore need of the larger chance; nothing quite so delightful as putting one who craves music, art, books, nature, in the way of enjoying these things. In a thousand ways life gains sweetness through the consciousness of the ability to do small kindnesses, to render minor services, to exercise a little thoughtfulness and courtesy. But no one has a right to take this pleasure to himself and deny it to others ; to insist upon giving, and at the same time refuse to receive. He only truly gives who receives as generously as he bestows. He who gives lavishly to me, but refuses to allow me to give to him, declares to all the world that he recognizes his own stewardship of all that he possesses, but denies mine ; he affirms his own duty, but ignores mine. This means the division of a responsibility which ought to rest whole and entire on all men and women. It is, at bottom, disloyalty to the principle that we are children of one Father, members of one household, and heirs of one estate. It is a false idea of independence which makes a man unwilling to lay himself under obligations to others. It is, to begin with, impossible for any man to live and avoid putting himself under the heaviest obligations. Everything has been done for us before we are born : life, law, nature, God first ; then society, government, school ; then art, literature, pleasure, and profit in countless forms — all these await a man when he arrives, naked, helpless, and ignorant, at the gate of the world. At the very beginning he is so loaded down with obligations that, no matter how great his services and how long and arduous his life, he goes out of the world hopelessly in debt to his fellows. But the world is not a place of barter, hard as some men strive to make it such ; it is a vast school, on a divine foundation, where everything is given in order that it may be given again. Every pupil who learns his lesson gives and takes with equal pleasure.

THE BETTER WAY

THE ideal life, as most men and women think of it, would be one utterly free from all claims upon time and resources which would check its movement, dwarf its growth, or impede its swift and orderly progress. Most of the rebellion against our circumstances arises from the feeling we have that they restrict, limit, and narrow us ; we should like to be set free, and we fancy that if no responsibilities or duties were imposed upon us other than those we choose for ourselves, we should move swiftly and irresistibly forward, accomplishing all our purposes and turning all our dreams into facts. But the divine way of obtaining freedom is very different from the human way. There is no truth which men and women accept so slowly and with so much pain of heart and mind as the truth that freedom comes through patience, and that our life gets its richness and strength, not by working itself out according to our plans, but by submitting itself to the direction of another. Every one of us has some little structure which he would like to complete for himself, laying the foundations, building the walls, spreading the roof, and adorning it without and within according to his own design. But God sets us at work upon an edifice so vast that our work upon it is only a small detail, and we are such inferior artists that we would prefer to be the architects of the small design rather than the builders of the great temple. There is not one of us upon whom some kind of restriction is not laid ; not one of us whose free, spontaneous movement of life is not checked by the weakness of some other whose work we have to add to our own. While we are doing the work of the day with all our might and with entire success, some one else near to us falls by inefficiency or by positive evil of nature, and we are obliged to stop and add his load to our own. Instead of doing the thing we would like, which would bring completeness to our life in our eyes, we must pick up a wearisome burden that has no inspiration in it, and carry it with a constant fear of loss. Many a woman's life would be far richer in her external activities and opportunities if she were not taking upon her own shoulders the deficiencies and weaknesses of others; many a man would have larger education, more congenial social surroundings, a sweeter life, if it were not for the responsibilities he assumes for those who are unable or unwilling to meet their own responsibilities. There are times when the best nature revolts against this apparent waste; and yet it is precisely through this discipline that men and women are molded into nobler spiritual stature; it is by patient submission to restriction, by cheerful bearing of the burdens of others, by uncomplaining acceptance of conditions imposed upon us by the weaknesses and sin of those that we love, that the truest liberty and the most enduring strength are won. Christ's life was the very opposite of that which, from any human conception, a divine nature would seek for itself; and yet it is plain that its highest divinity lay in its cheerful surrender to the hardness and barrenness of human conditions. He came not to be ministered unto, but to minister, and He saved His life by losing it.